Sharing the Journey

Spiritual Assessment and Pastoral Response
to Persons with Incurable Illnesses

Cornelius J. van der Poel, C.S.Sp.

A Liturgical Press Book

THE LITURGICAL PRESS
Collegeville, Minnesota

Cover design by Carol Weiler.

1   2   3   4   5   6   7   8   9

Library of Congress Cataloging-in-Publication Data

Poel, Cornelius J. van der, 1921–
    Sharing the journey : spiritual assessment and pastoral response
to persons with incurable illnesses / Cornelius J. van der Poel.
        p.   cm.
    Includes bibliographical references.
    ISBN 0-8146-2394-8 (alk. paper)
    1. Church work with the terminally ill.   2. Church work with the
terminally ill—Catholic Church.   3. Catholic Church—Clergy.
4. Terminally ill—Pastoral counseling of.   I. Title.
BV4460.6.P64   1998
259'.4175—dc21   97-27329
                                                            CIP

Contents

Acknowledgments

I want to express my most sincere gratitude to all who have collaborated in any way to the writing of this book. In particular I want to mention my students at Barry University who utilized and evaluated the instrument in their pastoral contact with patients. Further I want to express my sincere thanks to Revs. Henry J. Koren, C.S.Sp., and David C. Marshal, C.S.Sp., for their painstaking reading and critiquing of the manuscript. Without the help of all these friends the book would never have been written.

Foreword

The story goes that someone said to a friend: "Please, don't ask me to lead you, I feel too insecure to do that. And don't ask me to follow you, I may not be able to keep up with you. Just walk at my side as a friend and share my journey with me."

This was the experience of the two disciples on their way to Emmaus. Jesus fell in step with them, listened to their crisis of faith: their experience of joy and hope when the preacher from Nazareth convinced them that the messianic time was at hand, the bitter disillusionment with the condemnation and death of Jesus and now the confusing rumors of his resurrection. Jesus guided them from their limited understanding of the Scriptures to the fullness of the messianic revelation. Then, when they recognized Jesus in the breaking of the Bread, Jesus disappeared from their sight but left within their hearts the fire that started burning when he accompanied them on their journey and explained the Scriptures to them. They could not wait to share their new-found knowledge, security and joy with their friends in Jerusalem and returned that same night. The stranger who accompanied them became their guide to wholeness.

I read in this story of Luke the task of the chaplain or of any spiritual guide. There is the readiness to listen attentively to the crisis and the pain of the person "with whom we fall into step." When the depth of the pain and crisis has been revealed, the chaplain joins in the journey that searches for a personal wholeness in which this individual can fully respond to God's call in his or her present situation.

The instrument for spiritual assessment presented in this book intends to assist in this task. It makes the chaplain fall into step with the patient or directee to journey together toward a degree of wholeness in which patient or directee can live at this moment. The instrument is not a questionnaire. The last thing a patient, any patient, needs is another questionnaire. In the final analysis, to hand out a questionnaire reduces a person to an object of study. This instrument directs itself to the chaplain to create in his or her mind a framework of thought and perception in which the patient or directee can be understood as fully as possible at this moment. With this new insight the chaplain or director can join the patient as a friend on the journey toward wholeness after a crisis caused through accident or illness.

The instrument looks at the whole person in his or her self-perception, relationship to family and friends, participation in the life of church or society and in relationship to God. This vision of the current totality reveals strengths and weaknesses, doubts and confusion, traps and obstacles, often hidden from the patient, but that pose dangers on the road to wholeness.

Gentleness, understanding, and patience must guide the loving concern of chaplain or director and convey to the patient or directee the trust to listen to God's voice that speaks in the circumstances of their life, and that gives the courage to follow the road God maps out as a way toward wholeness.

Before using this instrument I suggest reading the book, pondering over its content, and assimilating it as much as possible at this time. Subsequent and frequent use will show its versatility and helpfulness. Although the book may give the impression that the instrument is primarily intended for ministering to incurably ill persons, acquaintance with it will show its usefulness for ministry to short-term patients as well. Obviously, when one can use it over a longer period of time with the same patient, it will provide much deeper insights, and it will show the growth and unfolding of the person. However, even for a one-time use it can be an invaluable framework for ministry with short-term patients. Some may even find it useful for ordinary spiritual direction.

The instrument approaches a person as created in the image of God and tries to assist the individual to manifest God's life and love in the reality of everyday activity and relationships, whether it be in health or in illness.

Introduction

In the early 1980s one of my students described ministry as an activity that enables others to act and to express themselves more effectively. This student grasped well my emphasis that ministry is not merely "doing things" for people but enabling individuals "to be their full self." In general I agree with this definition, but its meaning will vary greatly according to the needs of people. In the following pages my focus will be on a special perspective of ministry, namely, on the spiritual assessment of persons with incurable illnesses.

This special focus is, in my view, very important. In pastoral ministry to the sick we serve people whose life and self-expression have been seriously interrupted. However, in most instances they are persons who hope for a restoration of at least a certain degree of wholeness to their life and activities. In people with incurable illnesses this hope for "normalcy" is absent, yet, such people need ministry more than others. Pastoral ministry concerns itself with the whole person and wants to participate in a teamwork of holistic health care in which its special contribution lies in the area of spiritual care. In any form of treatment, the healer must make a diagnosis. A physician needs to know the place and the kind of discomfort a patient experiences. Without such knowledge a physician cannot even start thinking about medication or treatment. The expression "Take two aspirins and see me in the morning" does not sound very professional. For spiritual care also, a diagnosis or assessment is needed for responsible and effective treatment.

Spiritual assessment is an important element in the pastoral care of any person. It becomes more important when a person is ill. It becomes essential when a person is incurably ill and his or her condition becomes terminal. For this person physical health does not offer a viable prospect, human relationships undergo a radical change, and the final union with God is almost tangibly close. There is a difference between pastoral care for the dying and for the incurably ill. For the purpose of this study we may overlook this difference and focus on the spiritual assessment of persons with incurable illness whose life is running inevitably toward its conclusion. Yet, even in such circumstances there is a struggle for wholeness and an effort for self-realization despite their limitations. A struggle for life is always meaningful, a struggle against death is meaningless.[1]

Spiritual assessment says little, if anything, about dying, yet there are a few points about dying that strongly influence the meaning of spiritual assessment and pastoral guidance. These points need to be present in the mind of the pastoral worker.

1. Dying is a natural and inescapable human experience.

Every material existence is subject to decay and disappearance. Even the hardest rock changes under the influence of rain, storm, and earthquake. The human being is no exception. The very fact that there is a material element in human existence makes the person subject to decline and eventual disappearance from the material world. Nature itself condemns a person to death as Socrates interestingly remarked. When he was told "The thirty Tyrants have condemned you to death," he replied "And nature, them."[2] There is, however, a significant difference between the disintegration of a rock or the death of a plant or animal and the death of a human being. When the physical existence disintegrates, the rock or the plant has simply disappeared as such and continues to exist in the form of dust or another substance.

---

[1] *Care of the Dying. A Catholic Perspective* (St. Louis: CHA, 1993) vii.
[2] Joseph Telushkin, *Jewish Wisdom* (New York: William Morrow, 1994) 257.

The human being is a unique integration of material, psychological, and spiritual dimensions that together form an indivisible wholeness. When the physical existence disintegrates the earthly existence ceases, but the human being somehow continues to exist in a form that escapes our human intelligence. Catholic teaching, expressed in the *Catechism of the Catholic Church* explains that "death is the end of earthly life" (#1007) and that "by death the soul is separated from the body, but in the resurrection God will give incorruptible life to the body" (#1016). These statements do not explain the mystery of dying. Whatever approach or theory we may accept is not very important at this point. We need to keep two points in mind: (1) that dying is an unavoidable experience in human existence, and that (2) it is the most radical change ever to take place in human life. It is a change that affects the human in his or her totality of material, psychological, and spiritual existence.

2. Dying is a personal experience.

When Maximillian Kolbe offered himself to be executed in place of another condemned person, he underwent death for the other but not in such a way that the other person would never have to die. At the proper time everyone will. No one can substitute for another but everyone must personally go through the experience of dying.

Everyone will die according to one's circumstances and condition of life. Every person will experience his or her dying in the light of one's cultural, educational, and religious perspectives on life. Some look at death very quietly as a normal experience. That was the case of the gentleman for whom I, as missionary in Africa, was called to administer the sacraments of the sick. His house was more than two hours walk from the rectory along narrow, hilly footpaths in the scorching sun.

When I arrived at the village there was an old man sitting in front of his house and some younger people working close by. At my question where the sick person was, the old man answered, "That's me." After the exhausting walk I felt as if somebody played a trick on me and I said: "Well you don't look too sick to me." He replied "Father, I am going to die very soon." Out of respect for the two-hour walk in the burning sun, I administered the sacraments and went home. The next day I got the news that the gentleman had died during the night. Dying was for him a normal part of life.

3. Dying is an experience of the whole person.

We are used to the expression that the human being is soul and body and that in death these two "parts" are separated. What happens in the person is not explained. Dying is a mystery, not so much because soul and body are separated but rather because the human person who lives in the material world as an integrated wholeness of material, psychological, and spiritual dimensions, now continues to live in a radically different way. Although seemingly only the physical aspects have changed, the relationship between the psychological and spiritual aspects has gone through a radical change as well. The dying process has affected his or her total personality in every aspect. We can, therefore, expect in the dying and in the terminally ill person special psychological and spiritual needs as well.

The discussion of a theology of dying and death is beyond the scope of these pages. The important (and pastoral) factor is that the minister keep in mind that the patient faces the most radical change of his or her whole life and that ministry must respond to this looming presence of death while helping the person to live at this moment in a way that is most meaningful and effective for the individual.

In this light the necessity of a spiritual assessment becomes clearer. The patient is called to give a response to God in a way that is very different from any earlier response. The patient is in a stage of his or her journey to God where guidance is more needed than ever. It is the minister's task to join in this journey at the point where the patient is.

The Nature of Spirituality and Its Place in Human Life

The nature of spirituality and its place in human life is not understood in the same way by everyone. To avoid misunderstandings I use this first chapter to explain the nature of spirituality and its place in human life as it will be used in the development of the instrument for assessment and its pastoral application.

Spirituality is not an easy word to define because it deals with a concept and with a reality that escape tangible measurements. Yet it is a reality in human life. Most, if not all, religions consider it the center of human life and teach that it must be realized within human existence. In this study I am not concerned with the teachings of various schools of spirituality but with the everyday experience of people who try to make sense out of their life and give meaning to the painful conditions to which they are subjected.

The shortest, descriptive definition of spirituality possible states that spirituality is the personal attitude and behavior with which an individual responds to God.

This definition emphasizes three elements:

1. *Personal attitude* = the person's internal disposition and direction in relation to God;

2. *Personal behavior* = the external expression of this attitude, translating the internal disposition into visible activity;

3. *Individual's response to God* = the clarification or deepest meaning of the source and moti-
vation for one's external activity.

These three elements help us in our discussion of the nature of spirituality.

The Nature of Spirituality

Spirituality is not a result of reasoning. It is a reality that is built within the human person by the fact of being created in the image of God. If one denies being "created in the image of God," spirituality receives a very different meaning. Such persons, particularly atheists and agnostics, do not want to speak about spirituality. However, somewhere deep within them they usually recognize a value or principle that gives a unifying and meaningful direction to their life and activities. In this study I speak primarily about persons who accept the existence of God, but I will apply the principles, whenever possible, to assist others as well.

I start from the premise that human beings are created in the image of God. In earlier writings I have discussed this concept at length.[1] At this moment I want to emphasize only a few aspects.

"Being created" says that human beings do not suddenly appear spontaneously or by accident. It indicates that there is a source for their origin and that they have an innate dependency that ultimately falls back on a First Cause which we identify by the name of God. Being created "in the image of God" states that this dependency contains the task of expressing in the human reality a created manifestation of the Creator.

I understand creation as (1) a form of self-communication whereby the deepest layers of one's being are expressed in a new and original manner so that a new being that did not exist before comes into existence, and (2) reaching out or offering oneself in a constructive manner, i.e., in a manner in which an-

---

[1] *The Search for Human Values* (New York: Paulist, 1971), especially chapters I and II.

other (dependent) being gains in wholeness. In either case the created being reflects the inner self of the creator.

Consequently, the condition of being created indicates

1. Existing through the will and action of another,

2. Existing for the purpose that the other (creator) places within the creature,

3. Being neither the origin nor the goal of one's own existence,

4. Finding wholeness and completion in fulfilling the purpose and goal that the creator built within the creature,

5. Reflecting the nature of the creator through the constructive activation of one's created potential.

Being created in the image of God will then mean that

- God (the creator) who is the source of our being is also the purpose and fulfillment of our existence,

- God placed the purpose of our being within us,

- This purpose is being the image of God,

- This image contains (a) reaching out constructively, in a manner that is beneficial for the wholeness of self and others, (b) utilizing or unfolding the potential that is placed within us, (c) being open to receive from others, and (d) finding fulfillment in the positive unfolding of others,

- The creature must recognize, according to its own ability, its dependence on the Creator,

- The achievement of this wholeness is the fulfillment of the purpose that is built into the creature.

The manner in which the response to God, the creator and source of being, is expressed is called spirituality.

Human existence, created in the image of God, exists in a material world but cannot be described exclusively in material terms. We can consider a person from three perspectives: physical, psychological, and spiritual existence.

1. *Physical existence* describes the material, tangible, visible, measurable condition of the human presence in the world or in time and space. The "physical" is the basis and the surroundings within which human awareness develops. Through one's physical presence one can know (a) where one is at a certain moment, (b) what one looks like, (c) what one's abilities, strengths and weaknesses are, and (d) what the external qualities are of one's relationship to others, etc. The physical existence is an indispensable element in our self-knowledge and is extremely closely related to our identity as persons. Without a physical presence the human person cannot have a self-awareness in this world.

Physical existence by itself is not human existence. Human material must be activated or animated by psychological and spiritual dimensions. However, awareness, relationships and values can be expressed visibly and tangibly only through material existence. Physical existence is, therefore, more than a part of human existence; it is more than an aspect of being human. Physical existence is human existence from the perspective of existing in time and space. Because of physical existence, human beings are also subject to all cosmic laws of growth, development and decline.

2. *Psychological existence* is in itself not material but cannot exist in this world except by activating and animating a material being. The psychological existence is the human source of individual self-awareness. Through one's psychological qualities a person is able to experience one's own being, to develop a sense of personal value and dignity, and to relate to others by consciously reaching out to others and receiving from them. This process of self-realization can take the form of constructive growth or destructive decline.

Psychological existence is a relational quality that includes the emotional and social aspects of human existence. This, too, is more than a part of human reality; it is more than an aspect. Rather it is human existence itself from the perspective of personal and interpersonal relationships. Together with the physical elements the psychological existence constitutes the human existence in this world with all its intra-worldly potential. Yet, this intra-worldly potential does not depict the total human being. This kind of existence is held in common with animals, except for intellectual development, which is in humans usually higher, but this intellectual potential also is dependent on physical conditions. We may say that the psychological existence is not a separate existence, but it elevates physical reality to a higher level.

3. *Spiritual existence* is still more difficult to pinpoint than the psychological. The psychological is observable through attitudes and behavior and, as a consequence, it can be described, studied, and measured, at least to a certain extent. Spiritual existence escapes this possibility. What it does is to give to the physical and psychological dimensions a value and dignity that places them above their own natural level and makes them participants in the life of God. This does not happen on created merits but by the fact of being "inspirited" with a divine dignity.

The whole human being, as we know it in this world, is based in the material existence, finds its identity through psychological and spiritual perspectives, but *within* the material setting and relationships. Therefore, although spiritual dimensions are neither material nor psychological, they can be expressed in human existence only within the parameters of material reality.

The spiritual is not a third dimension alongside the physical and psychological. Rather, it permeates and embraces the whole human reality and enables it to exist as a wholeness created "in the image of God." Because humanity is created in the image of God, the spiritual dimension is a natural element in human existence. In other words, it is natural for the human being to be spiritual.

From a Christian point of view, spirituality is a personal assimilation of the salvific mission of Christ by each Christian. This assimilation must always be in the framework of new forms of Christian conduct. It is comprised within the fundamental answer of the Church to the word of salvation.[2] Since we are dealing with a "personal" assimilation, the personality of the individual will be of primary importance. Therefore, spirituality cannot be properly understood or evaluated unless we have some understanding of the conditions and needs of the individual whose spirituality we want to assess. The personality itself does not produce any spiritual condition or effect, but all concrete spiritual perspectives of life are expressed according to the ability and personality of the person who expresses them. Concrete spiritualities should be grasped less as doctrine than as personal experiences.[3] This means that spirituality is an aspect in which an individual *as person*, relates to God and spiritual values. No created reality can claim its own existence. Existence is always a gift. However, material and psychological existence fall within the realm of created existence, while spiritual existence surpasses created existence and participates in the divine being.

Spirituality is usually understood from the perspectives of certain schools of spirituality such as Ignatian, Franciscan, and Dominican. These reflections do not intend to give an understanding of any of these schools. Our concern is the understanding of the religious perspectives, values, and motivations that determine an individual's approach to life and that contribute to the shape of his or her responses to the demands and problems of daily existence.

Our reflections focus on the relationship with God in individual patients. Sometimes patients may not have any "admitted" relationship with God. Perhaps their attitude toward God is indifference, dislike, or even hatred, yet, deep within is the experience of a higher power that controls their life and may lead them to places where they do not want to go. In the daily human attitude toward God there are three major perspectives that describe to some degree the individual's relationship with "this power" beyond their control:

1. The form and degree of acceptance of a power beyond their control and the basic attitude toward it.

[2] *Sacramentum Mundi*, vol. 6 (New York: Herder & Herder, 1970) 149.
[3] Ibid., 151.

2. The degree (if any) of expectations with regard to this power. Does it care, does it respect human existence? Does it help and protect us?

3. The form of the human response to this power. Is it a willing cooperation or perhaps a dislike and rebellion?

These three basic attitudes represent, in common Christian perspective, the virtues[4] of faith, hope, and love. I want to study how these virtues tend to be present and operate in the daily life of an individual. These virtues form the basis of the human relationship with God and, therefore, are the object of the following discussion on the place of spirituality in human life.

The Place of Spirituality in Human Life

Spirituality is not merely an attitude. It is more than an attitude since it expresses a fundamental direction of the individual's existence. It is a personal perspective by which an individual is called to a form of self-realization that is unique and cannot be duplicated by anyone else. St. Francis de Sales brings it back to the process of creation in which God commanded that the plants of the earth bring forth fruit in accordance with their own kind. The goal of human existence is the self-fulfillment according to God's plan that is contained in the human abilities.[5] Thus the acts which the individual performs show how this person expresses his or her relationship with God in accordance with the personality and potential of the individual.

Spirituality is not produced by created human qualities. Human relationship to God is a divine gift. However, this relationship is created into the human reality and, therefore, it

[4] In this context and in further parts of this book, "virtue" is understood as a "successful human self-realization." I.e., the best available utilization of our "God-given" capacities for the fulfillment of our human capacities in relation to others and to God.

[5] St. Francis de Sales. *Introduction to the Devout Life.* See: Liturgy of the Hours, vol. III, January 24, 1,317.

belongs to the human wholeness. It must be expressed and lived in human fashion and within human dimensions. Hence, the human personality plays an important role in this relationship, since it is the shape in which the relationship to God finds a concrete realization. Spirituality follows the same pattern of development as any other dimension of human life; namely, it grows and develops with the personality in its connection with other persons. It declines and dies when it is neglected.

In this light we can begin to reflect on the place and task of the human qualities that underlie the relationship to God and the virtues that grow and develop together with these qualities.

FAITH

One of the deepest needs, if not *the* deepest need, in human self-realization is a sense of being personally acceptable to oneself and to others. Without this sense of acceptability, there is an emptiness in the individual. The absence of a sense of acceptability creates an irresistible tendency to fill this emptiness with activities or demands of another nature.

This sense of acceptability originates in the earliest stages of human life and corresponds to the degree in which the newborn experienced acceptance by his or her parents and significant others. This sense of acceptability lies at the basis of the person's self-acceptance, self-esteem and self-value and, consequently, it sets the tone and offers the shape for human relationships with others and ultimately for the human relationship with God.

Although the relationship with God cannot originate from human qualities, it is necessarily expressed and manifested in human qualities, abilities and activities. Faith has two aspects in the mind and feeling of the individual: (a) what God means to the individual, and (b) how the individual sees him or herself in relation to God. In the human developmental process the tension between Basic Trust vs. Basic Mistrust[6] creates a

---

[6] My approach to the development of the personality is largely based upon the eight psycho-social stages as developed by Eric Erikson.

corresponding degree of self-acceptance or non-acceptance. This degree in turn determines to what extent personal values are seen as being based within the individual or whether they must come from outside. This developmental stage is the basis for interhuman relationships. This same personality construct will be the basis for the human relationship with God. It will determine whether there is inner personal value that makes a person feel acceptable to God (even if this value is God's gift) or whether an individual feels that he or she must prove to God one's personal value through activities in order to gain acceptability.

HOPE

Hope contains many of the same qualities as faith, primarily (1) acceptance of one's total dependence on God, (2) acceptance of one's personal value before God. In addition, however, hope includes the acceptance that self-realization allows us to become what we are called to be, and that the human reality is acceptable before God. Hope deals with expectations that can be realized through serious application of human efforts and with the security that human activity is acceptable before God despite its many deficiencies.

The nature of hope brings us back to an early stage of human development in which a child begins to act on its own. Eric Erikson calls this "Autonomy vs. Shame." The child's lack of knowledge, experience, and insight may cause clashes with the adult world. Depending on the nature and severity of such clashes, a child will get the message whether it may or may not "realize itself." If it may, the child will look forward to collaborating with the adult world. If it may not it will try to seek its own way despite the adult world. The ability to collaborate is enhanced by and will enhance the self-image and self-esteem in relation to other persons.

A similar development can be expected in relationships with God. Our human activity has necessarily a relation to God. Whether this activity is considered to be acceptable will depend on whether the individual feels acceptable as a person. The sense of personal unacceptability creates the feeling of being unacceptable before God and, as a consequence, feeling rejectable before God, but being unacceptable before God increases the feeling of personal rejectability. The relationship to God is shaped in accordance with the human personality. Thus faith and hope are strongly interrelated because of the many corresponding characteristics and because of their close relationship to the structure of the personality.

LOVE

Love is the human capacity to extend and activate the best of one's qualities (oneself) for the good of another. It is a giving of self to others. Love presupposes a healthy self-acceptance as well as an ability to cooperate with others. A person with a poor self-image is afraid or ashamed to present oneself to another as a gift. The self-accepting person can take the initiative and feel assured that he or she will be acceptable. Whenever an individual does not have this sense of personal value, every action with relation to others will be an effort to gain the other's approval. It will be a taking-possession of the other for one's own enrichment rather than a contribution to the growth of the other. Such actions are in the final analysis a self-seeking performance, however generous they may look from the outside. There is an unspoken condition attached to such activities, namely, "I do this for you, but I expect to be rewarded for doing it." To the degree that a person feels accepted for one's own sake, to that same degree can one extend oneself unconditionally to other persons.

The human interaction is again the mold in which one's relationship with God will receive a concrete form. If there is no personal value, an individual cannot believe to be accepted and loved for one's own sake. Such a person must "perform" in order to gain acceptance, and the love for God needs to be a "performance" (an activity) in order to be acceptable. The activity that is meant to be a sign of one's love for God becomes a payment to earn acceptability.

In these three aspects of faith, hope and love, we see, therefore, a strong correlation between the personality structure and the human relationship with God. We must keep in mind, however, that relationship with God does not originate from the personality but is only expressed in the form which the personality and one's responsibilities allow. St. Francis de Sales points out in his *Introduction to the Devout Life* that the spiritual practices of a bishop and of a Carthusian must be different, the spiritual life of a married person must be different from that of a monk. Personality and responsibility give form and depth to one's spirituality, although spirituality is always God's gift to individual and community. This helps us to see the place of spirituality in human life, namely, as the fulfillment of one's personality as it reaches beyond oneself to others and beyond the material world into God.

It is important not to judge individuals according to the extent or degree of their ability to accept God unconditionally and to respond to God with full personal dedication. As chaplains and spiritual guides, we may never attach guilt to a seemingly lesser form of dedication. The degree of self-giving that a person displays at a certain moment will be the place where the person is at that moment and, consequently, this is also the place from where he or she must start journeying to God. It is also the place where the chaplain can join in the journey with the individual. A method of "how to find this place" is presented in the next chapter.

2

The Assessment of Spirituality

Chapter 1 indicates the close interaction between the physical-psychological condition of an individual and the expression of a person's relationship with God. However, we cannot assess a patient's relationship with God by simply evaluating the individual's psychological condition. Although the psychological structure is the shape through which spiritual values and the human relationship with God will be expressed, it cannot be equated with these values and relationships.

> Psychological structures are not a personal choice, but one's relationship with God is the individual's personal choice and responsibility within the limits of one's intellectual and emotional abilities.

A healthy and theologically sound relationship with God will have a positive, strengthening, and healing influence upon a person's psychological structure, while an unhealthy and theologically unsound relationship with God will have a negative and harmful influence upon the individual's psychological condition. For example, a sense of insecurity and rejection resulting from early childhood experiences will slowly be healed when faith brings the person in touch with a loving and accepting God. But a sense of personal rejection will deepen when God is presented and understood as unloving and punitive. In this case the healing process can be seriously hindered.

Contact with many people tells us that persons who have experienced childhood rejection, or who feel abandoned by others, will be inclined to see God as stern, revengeful and punitive, while persons who feel personally acceptable will be more inclined to see God as good and accepting. Therefore, the deeper the chaplain's insight and understanding of an individual's psychological condition and spiritual approach, the more effective pastoral care is likely to be. For this reason an effective spiritual assessment must take into consideration a general insight into the patient's physical and psychological condition as well since the physical, psychological, and spiritual dimensions strongly interact and do not act independently.

An assessment is by nature tentative and may never be judgmental. It may not place people in "spiritual pigeonholes." The assessment is intended to suggest the current human-spiritual balance[1] that the patient experiences in the present circumstances of his or her life. The balance of the current physical, psychological, and spiritual dimensions suggests the point of departure where the pastoral minister can join a patient on his or her spiritual journey. This point of departure can be found only by very careful and delicate conversations that evaluate the present condition of the individual and his or her relationship to God and neighbor.

It is my view that a spiritual assessment cannot be deducted from the person's stated or confessed relationship to God without an understanding of his or her relationship and attitude toward self, others, and community. All these relationships are inseparably interwoven. In developing a spiritual assessment I tried to take these relationships into account by including in the conversation the person's relationship to self, to others and to God, so that all major tendencies of the individual are evaluated.

The methodology is quite simple:

   a. The assessment instrument contains five general questions which are important to gain an insight into the individual's tendency with regard to his or her basic attitude toward life and toward God.

[1] The word "balance" indicates the state in which the physical, psychological and spiritual tendencies of the person create a condition/relationship of inner peace and acceptability.

These five general questions deal with:

1. The place of God in the patient's life;
2. The patient's attitude toward him or herself;
3. The patient's relationship with family and friends;
4. The patient's understanding of and interest in prayer;
5. The patient's attitude toward his or her religious denomination or church.

b. To answer these five questions each of them is assessed by four sub-statements that focus on several perspectives of the general statement and indicate into what direction the individual's (spiritual) tendencies seem to lean;

c. Each sub-statement is evaluated on a scale from 1–5 (strong disagreement to strong agreement) which indicates the apparent strength or intensity of each specific tendency.

Let me describe the meaning of each question and its substatements.

1. How does the patient see the place of God in his or her life?[2]

Through this statement I try to discover what the patient's understanding is of God. The word God can have many meanings.[3] I see three general ways in which people understand God. For some people God is someone who can only be pleased and satisfied by ritual performances that border on magical forces. We see this, for instance, in persons who dare not to be seated in row thirteen on a plane, or take a room on the thirteenth floor of a hotel, or call off their trip when a black cat has

---

[2] The complete instrument for assessment is given at the end of this chapter. At this point I present and explain each individual statement to clarify its value in the assessment process.

[3] For more detailed explanation on the various understandings of God, see my *The Search for Human Values* (New York: Paulist, 1971) 16–20.

crossed the road in front of them, or who dare not go into the street without wearing a fetish (or medal) to be sure of God's protection.

Other people look at God in a more *religious* way. For them God is something like a master puppeteer who is responsible for every single move the puppets make. Nothing in life happens without God explicitly willing it. The person is responsible for every individual act, and God keeps count of both the good and bad performances. God is a cold-hearted law-giver who demands perfect submission to, and fulfillment of all commandments and who rewards accordingly, but who has little further interest in what happens to human beings. Others see God in a more *dynamic* way. God is seen and understood as the creator and concerned companion who is always with us in joy and in pain, and who is a partner in human life so that in everyday human existence the loving God and the human person form, as it were, one principle of operation.

Such various approaches and attitudes never exist in their undiluted and pure form. In every person is always some mixture of inclinations, but there will almost always be a general leaning toward one direction or another. The care-giver should not judge which direction is good or bad. The care-giver must meet the patient where the patient is in order to speak the same language and to be an effective guide or support for this person. To impose one's own concept of God upon the patient would be a serious disservice and injustice, particularly when a patient is already under heavy stress.

These various tendencies may have a greater or lesser intensity in the patient. Their intensity influences the patient's behavior and attitude in other areas of life. These attitudes are captured in four brief statements and each of them is evaluated on an intensity-scale of 1 (lowest intensity) to 5 (highest intensity).

    a. Everything that happens in my life is explicitly willed by God.

       1   2   3   4   5

b. God is sort of a partner in my life. He is involved in all that I do.

| 1 | 2 | 3 | 4 | 5 |

c. God is sitting on his throne high in the heavens with little concern about what goes on in human life.

| 1 | 2 | 3 | 4 | 5 |

d. God is more a demanding lawgiver than a loving Father.

| 1 | 2 | 3 | 4 | 5 |

The intensity and interaction of these statements will give a fairly accurate and workable vision on the patient's attitude toward God and religious values. The same basic concepts can be used also for persons who do not believe in God but who have some other principle or value that gives direction to their life.[4] That principle or value may be seen as the unifying factor for their self-realization and can offer an appropriate basis for pastoral guidance toward an inner peace.

The relationship to God can be expressed only in human concepts and in human terminology. Therefore, it is directly related to the individual's understanding and value of one's own personality. Thus the next point on which we need to focus is the patient's self-concept.

2. What is the main characteristic of the patient's attitude toward him or herself?

Every human relationship starts with a self-concept, even the relationship with oneself. We all have met people, or we know people who are afraid to appear in public because they feel that they will make a fool of themselves. They just are not made for that kind of activity. We know others who always are the center of attention in any company. As soon as the attention shifts to someone else they feel abandoned. They will try

---

[4] Almost all persons who claim to profess a form of atheism or agnosticism admit some central principle that gives meaning to their existence and activities. This principle forms a unifying factor for their self-realization.

hard to return to the center or withdraw in boredom and disgust. Others again feel that they have lost their personal value if they cannot be in control of their surroundings and the people around them. Others are satisfied and at peace in any situation. Whether they are center-stage or on the periphery does not disturb their self-respect and inner peace.

These few scenarios, obviously, do not exhaust all possible personality patterns. They do point out, however, that underneath all human behavior lies an urge or a need that drives a person into a certain direction. This undercurrent does not only affect interhuman behavior but also one's fundamental relationship to God, because this undercurrent guides people to produce a self-expression with which they are comfortable.

What holds true for interhuman relationships also holds true for relationships with God. In earlier writings I have explained how the shape of the personality is also the shape in which a person expresses him or herself with relationship to people and to God.[5] The creative tension between one's personality structure and one's external behavior has a strong influence upon one's ability to deal with suffering.[6] The most important factor is that when one comes to grips with the undercurrent of a person's self-concept, one gets a better insight into why this person relates to self and to God in the way he or she does.

Self-concept and attitude toward God are not only very closely related, they also interact very closely. For instance, a self-rejecting person will be inclined to feel rejectable before God as well, but he or she can gain in confidence and personal value when God is experienced as loving and caring. This same person can be pushed into a still greater depth of self-rejection when God is presented as punitive and demanding.

Another important factor is that a serious accident or illness, e.g., cancer or AIDS, includes almost unavoidably an attack on one's self-concept and self-value. Even a person with a healthy

---

[5] For the interaction between personality structure and attitudes towards God, see my *The Integration of Human Values* (Denville, N.J.: Dimension Books, 1977), especially 108–38.

[6] Cornelius van der Poel, *Growing Through Pain and Suffering* (Mystic, Conn.: Twenty-Third Publications, 1995) at various places.

self-esteem will be thrown off balance, at least temporarily, when faced with such painful conditions. A person who is thrown off balance, is most likely to fall back upon an earlier stage of emotional development that corresponds best to the present condition of ability and dependence. This involves no blame for the individual, it is merely a normal and healthy defense mechanism. Such a person will most likely pull out of it in a very short time, but the care-giver may not ignore the dynamics that are going on at that moment. In order to get a vision on the personality structure of the patient and the dynamics that are operative at that moment, the following statements and their degree of intensity offer a guideline.

a. A feeling of self-pity and/or disbelief that this could happen to him or her.

1   2   3   4   5

b. A feeling of self-rejection because all personal value is destroyed by the illness.

1   2   3   4   5

c. A feeling of inner peace and acceptance since he or she has handled many problems and God is always there as a partner and friend.

1   2   3   4   5

d. A feeling of anger with God and neighbor since all seem to have abandoned him or her.

1   2   3   4   5

The attitudes reflected in these statements go from angry self-rejection to peaceful self-acceptance. The degree of intensity helps to see where on this scale the patient may be. If one then compares the predominant concept of God with the predominant self-understanding, then one has the first step in the evaluation of the religious depth of this person and the first suggestion for a pastoral response.

There are, however, many other elements that enter into the personality structure that all contribute to the development of an appropriate approach for efficient pastoral care. One of the essential elements in the formation of the personality is the family relationship.

3. How can we best describe the patient's relationship with family and friends?

No human being can exist in a vacuum or in total isolation. This is true for the moment of birth as well as for the subsequent growth and development into maturity and for the maintenance of one's human wholeness during the gradual decline toward the completion of life. The individual's self-image and self-esteem, however, are inseparably connected with the earliest life experiences.

When a person has reached adulthood, we assume that an individual makes his or her personal and responsible decisions, independent from parental influences. In reality, however, the parental influences have created a tendency or mind-set that forms the basis for future direction in acting and decision-making. This earliest parental influence is not necessarily an iron grip that never lets go, but a certain influence will always remain. The strength and the form of this influence depends on the early freedom, respect, and encouragement (or the lack thereof) one has experienced. In normal circumstances, family and friends form a safe haven to which a person can retreat for relaxation and "refueling" or for support in times of stress.

Normally, family and friends form the first line of defense against loneliness and the feeling of abandonment. Thus the relationship with friends and family represent a significant source of information in evaluating an individual's personality structure. The knowledge about the family influence is particularly helpful for evaluating the person's self-image, his or her ability or manner of coping with difficulties, one's ability and form of relating to other people and relating to God. This does not mean that an individual will necessarily act (or believe) as the parents or family do. Sometimes people act or believe in the exact opposite way. It would not be surprising, however, if this "opposite way" were a reaction to earlier experiences or a defense mechanism to prove one's independence. In circumstances of great emotional stress, people often find security in the earlier stages of their relationships. The pastoral minister must meet them at the point where they are at this moment of need.

This family-and-friend relationship is not only a source of support for one's self-esteem and self-acceptance, it also influences or shapes one's ability to understand and to trust God. There is no need to psychoanalyze the patient, but some salient points of the early relationships shine through rather easily and can give some valuable hints:

a. A relationship of trust and mutual support.

    1   2   3   4   5

b. A relationship of mutual indifference.

    1   2   3   4   5

c. A friendly relationship but without warmth or closeness.

    1   2   3   4   5

d. A distant, mistrusting relationship in which the patient easily feels betrayed, rejected or abandoned.

    1   2   3   4   5

The interaction, emphasis, and intensity of the above feelings give a deeper insight into the patient's ability to establish closeness and to trust others. They give also an additional perspective into the potential of the patient's personal contribution in the healing process. Relationships with family and friends tell a lot about a person's self-image and about the availability of an emotional support system which is so important in the healing process. It also suggests how the patient's relationship with God is likely to be. This relationship with God, however, becomes clearer in the next two units. We first will look at the patient's personal feelings or relationship with God and his or her expectations of God, and later at the support that is expected from the Church or denominational community.

4. What is the patient's understanding of and interest in prayer?

As Christians we believe that faith is a gift of God, but it must be expressed through human qualities and abilities. This means faith will be expressed or lived according to the structure of the individual's personality. A person who has grown up in a loving, trusting environment has a good chance to become a trusting person and will usually find it easy to trust God. While the person who experienced harshness, rejection, abandonment, and distrust will most likely express some of these characteristics in his or her own life and will probably find it very difficult to trust God as well. The person who sees God primarily as "store-keeper and supplier" is inclined to ask and ask, while the person for whom God is a partner in life may rather see what "God and he or she" can do together about the situation. Some people seem to think that God owes them a few things, others are inclined to wait passively for God's intervention, while another category will seek ways to make of life what they can and see this as a collaboration with God.

The personal attitude toward life and toward God will be reflected in the manner people pray and in the influence prayer has on their life and behavior. This variety of attitudes is reflected in the following statements:

   a. Total indifference toward prayer. It has no meaning or benefit.

         1   2   3   4   5

   b. A means to ask (or plead with) God to give healing or at least to arrest the illness.

         1   2   3   4   5

   c. An angry rejection of prayer because despite all prayer the illness continues to ravage his/her health.

         1   2   3   4   5

   d. A source of strength which enables the patient to find union with God and consolation in suffering.

         1   2   3   4   5

In almost all circumstances the responses to these statements will reflect fairly accurately the tendencies of the personality and the person's understanding of God. A total indifference toward prayer may sometimes indicate a tendency toward atheism or agnosticism, but then it would be helpful to see if there is any central value that gives meaning and direction to life. It also may indicate a deep sense of frustration. It may suggest an attitude that expects that God will do exactly as one asks. The noncompliance on God's part proves God's anger or lack of concern. The focus on the attitude toward prayer does not intend to evaluate the frequency or fervor of a person's prayer. It is more concerned about what a person expects from God and how the relationship with God is understood. The attitude toward prayer also shows whether the individual's relationship with God is mostly individually oriented or whether the community plays a role in it.

5. What is the main characteristic of the patient's attitude toward his or her religious denomination or church?

Church, denomination, congregation, community all indicate a certain degree of connectedness on account of religious faith. The form and degree of connectedness varies greatly, not only from denomination to denomination but also within the same Church or denomination. To make the language a little easier I will use the word "church" to indicate any religious group.

The church is at the center of the life of many people, but it may be the center in different ways. Let me try to state the more significant meanings that people give to it.

1. Church may be the place where people go to worship on a more or less regular basis and, although many people may be present, most are and remain strangers to each other. Worship is often so individualized that group relationship and mutual support, if they exist at all, are minimal.

2. Church may also be a place where friends gather to worship together, to strengthen friendship, to find ways

to reach out to others in their joys and hardships. There is a mutual support that is carried primarily on the faith of the members.

3. Church may not so much be a place but rather a concept or an organization that represents God and religious values. The expectations that one has of such a church correspond largely to the expectations a person has of God. For some people it is a constant presence and encouragement, for others a sore in the community or perhaps a "non-entity." Accordingly individuals expect to be totally ignored or to find acceptance and emotional and spiritual support.

Since the church is often seen as the representation of God, recognition and acceptance by the church also means acceptance by God. One's relationship with the church is then experienced as an indicator of one's relationship with God. The various forms of involvement or connectedness with the church are captured in the following statements:

a. A feeling of respect and trust because of the community's or church's support.

| 1 | 2 | 3 | 4 | 5 |

b. A feeling of anger because of the church's indifference or the church's rejection of my situation.

| 1 | 2 | 3 | 4 | 5 |

c. Complete indifference because the church has nothing to offer.

| 1 | 2 | 3 | 4 | 5 |

d. An inner desire to belong to the church and be supported by it, but also a deep-seated fear of rejection.

| 1 | 2 | 3 | 4 | 5 |

These statements search for the individual's attitude toward the religious community to which he or she claims to belong. For many people the sense of belonging or not belonging to a church is an additional experience of personal value and of value before God. Thus it hooks up with the concepts of self-esteem and relationship with God. It completes the picture of the spiritual and personal condition of the patient and presents to the minister a tentative point of departure for pastoral care.

These five perspectives on the individual, the understanding of God, self-image, community relations, prayer, and religious affiliation, give an integrated vision of the person. All five perspectives are necessary for a valid spiritual assessment. Spirituality does not stand independent from the rest of the human person but must be integrated into human wholeness. Wherever and whenever this integration takes place, one can expect an impact of the spiritual dimension upon the bodily and psychological dimensions of the person. The influence of the spiritual dimension can then contribute to the healing process, or if the spiritual perspective is negative, it can influence the healing process negatively.

These are only a few of the many aspects that reveal something about the patient's relationship with God (or the value that guides his or her life). The assessment instrument that is presented here is not meant to be a questionnaire to be filled out by the patient. *It is intended to provide a backdrop and framework in the mind of the care-giver.* Any care-giver will, of course, form an opinion about the patient and will evaluate, approach, and treat the patient accordingly. This instrument suggests a framework that is simple enough for the ordinary person to understand and to incorporate into one's own way of thinking. It is also sophisticated enough to provide a valid professional evaluation. If it is used over a longer period of time, the instrument allows to see a change in the individual. It can provide a spiritual "progress-report" that makes the care-giver aware of the effectiveness of certain approaches. One possible method to see the process of development in the patient is to *color-code* one's assessment of the patient on a weekly basis on the same instrument sheet. This method would also show the possible need for change when values or needs shift in the patient.

It is most important, however, to remember that a spiritual assessment may NEVER take the form of investigative questioning. It must remain a sign and experience of *friendly concern*. The assessment should take the form of a conversation between chaplain and patient. Questions are asked and responses are given, but questions or responses do not offer any mathematical precision. Assessment does not *judge* presence or absence of a relationship with God. It only *establishes* presence or absence and the degree or intensity of such a relationship.

Let us take for example the first general question with its sub-statements as they might look when evaluating two individuals:

How does the patient see the place of God in his or her life?[7]

a. Everything that happens to me is explicitly willed by God.

1   2   <u>3</u>   4   **5**

b. God is sort of a partner in my life. He is involved in all that I do.

1   **2**   3   4   <u>5</u>

c. God is sitting high in the heavens with little concern about what goes on in human life.

<u>1</u>   2   3   **4**   5

d. God is more a demanding law-giver than a loving father.

1   <u>2</u>   3   **4**   5

The markings, (a) bold and (b) double underlined, which show in the numbers of the scale under the above statements, represent a chaplain's impression or assessment of how two (imaginary) individuals see the place of God in their lives.

Person A (bold) seems to have a rather austere vision of God. He or she seems to be convinced that God decides on every individual happening in life (a-5) with little personal concern for the individual (c-4). God is seen as a lawgiver (d-4)

---

[7] When dealing with patients who claim not to believe in any form of God, the chaplain may want to substitute (in his own mind) the word God with "highest value" or a similar concept.

with whom there is little collaboration but plenty of submission (b-2). The conversation with the individual will reveal other tendencies that strengthen and clarify the above impression. To speak with such a person about a loving God who forgives and is pleased when a person does the best he or she can do will most likely not be very effective. Initially there will be more need to show that God's law and God's actions are filled with love, even though we may not always understand how.

Person B (double underlining) looks at God differently. For this individual God is a deeply concerned person (c-1). Sure he or she must obey God's laws (d-2), but these laws are not an imposition. They rather are guidelines for our own good. God regulates everything in human life, but leaves room for human responsibility (a-3). God is first of all a partner with the human (b-5) in the living of human life. Personal and communal characteristics will most likely emphasize personal value and constructive relationships with other people. If this is correct, person B will have much more personal strength and many more community support systems than person A. An effective pastoral approach will have a very different focus for each individual.

Again I want to emphasize that an assessment never gives a mathematical precision. It provides an intelligent assumption that must prove itself in the course of action. The patient's condition and profile will change significantly when his or her condition improves or deteriorates. It will be the pastoral challenge to continue to evaluate and to adjust whenever changes take place and to guide the patient through all stages of the process toward healing or wholeness.

This also indicates how the instrument is to be used. As I mentioned earlier, the instrument is not a questionnaire that the patient has to fill out. The patient has enough tension already. Let us not add to it by handing out additional questionnaires. The instrument is meant to be a mental framework for the care-giver who can continue to fill in the gaps at every step of the illness.

The instrument itself may seem to lean heavily on psychology and personality structure. However, psychology alone can never give any answer about God's presence, except that it of-

Sources of Personal and Spiritual Relationships			
Relationship to	Characterized by	Degree/Scale 1–5	Originated from
Self	acceptance respect value rejection low esteem	_____ _____ _____ _____ _____	_____ _____ _____ _____ _____
Family/Friends	acceptance respect value low esteem defensive aggressive protective	_____ _____ _____ _____ _____ _____ _____	_____ _____ _____ _____ _____ _____ _____
Community/ Church	belonging involved passive indifferent hostile	_____ _____ _____ _____ _____	_____ _____ _____ _____ _____

God	legislator
	protector
	giver/worker
	  of all that
	  happens
	healer
	companion
	source of
	  strength
	peace
	presence
		_____
		_____
		
		_____
		_____
		_____
		
		_____
		_____
		_____
			_____
			_____
			
			_____
			_____
			_____
			
			_____
			_____
			_____

Prayer	petition submission very personal involves community frequent very seldom traditional spontaneous	_____ _____ _____ _____ _____ _____ _____ _____	_____ _____ _____ _____ _____ _____ _____ _____

fers the form and shape in which the relationship with God will be understood and lived. The relationship with God and spiritual values is explicitly contained in every statement and sub-statement of the instrument.

Although the full instrument is given below, I give on p. 36 another helpful means to assess the spirituality of the patient. This means uses a more psychological approach, but it leads to a deeper understanding of the human relationship to God. It is based upon the many relationships that exist in the individual and indicates where and how specific characteristics became part of the personality. This information can be most helpful for effective and individualized pastoral ministry.

These combined characteristics help us to see where the patient is and in which ways one may be able to provide pastoral assistance and guidance. This listing of characteristics and their origin may even serve as an assessment instrument, although personally I consider the following instrument much sharper to indicate the relationship with God and community.

Instrument for Spiritual Assessment

1. How does the patient see the place of God in his or her life?

a. Everything that happens in my life is explicitly willed by God.

1   2   3   4   5

b. God is sort of a partner in my life. He is involved in all that I do.

1   2   3   4   5

c. God is sitting on his throne high in the heavens with little concern about what goes on in human life.

1   2   3   4   5

d. God is more a demanding law-giver than a loving father.

1   2   3   4   5

2. What is the main characteristic of the patient's attitude toward him or herself?

a. A feeling of self-pity and/or disbelief that this could happen to him or her.

1   2   3   4   5

b. A feeling of self-rejection because all personal value is destroyed by the illness.

1   2   3   4   5

c. A feeling of inner peace and acceptance since he/she has handled many problems and God is always there as a partner and friend.

1   2   3   4   5

d. A feeling of anger with God and neighbor since all seem to have abandoned him/her.

1   2   3   4   5

3. How can the patient's relationship with family and friends best be described?

a. A relationship of trust and mutual support.

1   2   3   4   5

b. A relationship of mutual indifference.

1   2   3   4   5

c. A friendly relationship but without warmth or closeness.

1   2   3   4   5

d. A distant, mistrusting relationship in which the patient easily feels betrayed, rejected and abandoned.

1   2   3   4   5

4. What is the patient's understanding of and interest in prayer?

a. Total indifference since prayer has no meaning or benefit.

1   2   3   4   5

b. A means to ask (or plead with) God to give healing or at least to arrest the illness.

1   2   3   4   5

c. An angry rejection of prayer because despite all prayer the illness continues to ravage his/her health.

| 1 | 2 | 3 | 4 | 5 |

d. A source of strength which enables the patient to find union with God and consolation in suffering.

| 1 | 2 | 3 | 4 | 5 |

5. What is the main characteristic of the patient's attitude toward his or her religious community or church?

a. A feeling of respect and trust because of the community's/Church's support.

| 1 | 2 | 3 | 4 | 5 |

b. A feeling of anger because of the Church's indifference or the Church's rejection of my situation.

| 1 | 2 | 3 | 4 | 5 |

c. Complete indifference because the church has nothing to offer.

| 1 | 2 | 3 | 4 | 5 |

d. An inner desire to belong to the Church and be supported by it, but also a deep-seated fear of rejection.

| 1 | 2 | 3 | 4 | 5 |

These five general statements for the assessment cover the major areas of the patient's life. Through their differentiated strength the specific individual items indicate and help to assess the patient's attitudes toward self, life, and relationships. They give the chaplain a basis from where he or she can attempt to journey with the patient toward wholeness and peace.

Through the interaction of all five components, the religious profile of the patient will surface. This profile will not be absolute but merely a suggestion of the general approach to God and spiritual values of this person at this moment. It is, however, a sufficient basis for individualized pastoral care and spiritual guidance, provided the chaplain stays alert for changes due to altered circumstances, development and growth.

3

Psychological and Spiritual Needs of Persons with Incurable Illnesses

Psychological and spiritual needs are always particular and individual. Every individual has his or her personal approach to life and a personal value system. Even if people have the same religious denomination, their approach to individual cases and circumstances has always a personal tone that is different from other people. Consequently, it is impossible to compose a list of needs that can simply be applied to any individual.

There are, however, certain broad perspectives which allow us to place persons into larger groups in which, in individual instances, a certain kind of response or reaction is likely to occur. For instance, a person who is diagnosed with skin cancer will respond differently than a person who is diagnosed with HIV+. This broader "group-classification" allows us to develop a more individualized form of pastoral care without putting the patients in pigeon holes.

The system of such group-classification is common in the fields of medicine and psychology. We can find such general divisions, for instance, in the Diagnostic and Statistical Manual for Mental Disorders IV (DSM-IV). But even there the authors present a Cautionary Statement to remind the reader that the specific diagnostic criteria are offered as "guidelines for making diagnoses."[1]

---

[1] *Diagnostic and Statistical Manual of Mental Disorders,* Fourth edition (American Psychiatric Association, 1994) XXVII.

The same caution must be applied in the use of the Instruments for the Assessment of Spirituality. They help to develop a guideline. They do not give an absolute answer.

John Oldham and Lois Morris, in their book *The Personality Self-Portrait*[2] study thirteen distinct personality styles which they present as a counter balance against thirteen personality disorders given in the DSM-III-R. They show that these individual styles are not complete on their own but that the interaction between various styles leads to concrete individual personality styles. Such works as DSM and Personality Self-Portrait make it clear that the human physical condition has a great influence upon the psychological as well as spiritual responses and attitudes in a person.

Illness creates a "new" situation that changes the usual and familiar approach to life. The individual needs to "re-adjust" him or herself to new circumstances and find a new basis for their personal security. Quite often such persons fall back on an earlier successful defense mechanism where they felt safe and could live with themselves. This earlier point of security will be the starting point for the rebuilding of their self-esteem and to find a new balance in their life. For instance, when someone who never really felt accepted as a person but found security in excelling in tennis, loses a leg in an accident, this person loses also his or her sense of personal value and security. To find an immediate basis for security, this individual will fall back on an earlier form of behavior and on an earlier defense mechanism in order to find a personal balance and acceptability for this moment. It is from that vantage point that the patient will start rebuilding his or her self-esteem and that the chaplain or care-giver can join in the journey toward a new form of personal wholeness.

When people are ill they will react differently than they would if they were in good health (these differences are discussed in more detail in my *Growing Through Pain and Suffering*).[3]

[2] John M. Oldham and Lois B. Morris, *The Personality Self-Portrait. Why You Think, Work, Love and Act the Way You Do* (New York: Bantam Books, 1990).
[3] Mystic, Conn.: Twenty-Third Publications, 1995.

In this study I focus primarily on persons whose illness cannot be cured. This may include persons for whom death is imminent and others for whom death may not be in the picture at all. The instrument itself can be effective in the care of any patient, whether they go through a short-term hospital stay or whether they are there for extended care. My focus is on persons who need long-term care and whose condition is continually deteriorating. On the one hand, the care for such persons places higher demands on the care-giver, while on the other hand there is more time and opportunity to guide the patient in his or her personal growth process.

Even within this narrow field of incurable illnesses, there is a great variety of psychological and spiritual needs. Not only does each illness have its own particular needs, but within each illness there are many differentiations depending on the kind and degree of the debilitating nature of the illness and on the personality of the patient. It is impossible to study all the details of every illness. However, there are certain general perspectives that allow us to evaluate patients in larger groups where we can expect a similarity of responses in similar circumstances. Such similarities help us to decide what pastoral response would seem more beneficial at this moment, but, while focusing on the general nature of certain needs, we may not overlook the highly individual nature of the experience of suffering. The nature of the illness and the personality structure of the patient interact in their own way, create specific needs and place specific burdens upon patients. In this chapter I will first discuss some general characteristics in persons with incurable illnesses, thereafter I will discuss how these characteristics become more specific in particular illnesses.

I. *General characteristics and needs in patients with incurable illnesses*

Psychological and spiritual needs are not identical. They refer to different dimensions of the same person. However, they are also very much interwoven since the spiritual dimension expresses itself through psychological faculties. Spiritual needs ask for a certain degree of psychological functioning. They ask for a certain degree of personal choice and consent. In this section the major emphasis is placed on the psychological needs and from there reference is made to spiritual needs. The following listing of needs is not complete. It only intends to highlight and explain general needs and characteristics that usually occur.

A. Loss of Self-Esteem or Self-Value

Self-acceptance, self-esteem, self-image, or self-value are words that point to a fundamental attitude that lies at the basis of all human relationships. It includes the total personality: physical appearance and abilities, intellectual know-how and emotional experiences, and the human relationship with God. An inner satisfaction with "who one is" opens the way for a confident, balanced and peaceful approach to life and surrounding. An inner dissatisfaction prevents peace and balance in life. A few years ago a dark spot on my nose was diagnosed as melanoma, a malignant and dangerous kind of skin cancer. Walking around with a sizeable bandage on one's nose for about three months makes a person self-conscious. I did not appear in public places without a good reason. This experience is extremely minor. It is not like having an incurable illness such as cancer or AIDS, but it helps us to see how a minor external defect can affect a person's behavior.

Incurable illness alters the physical potential and prospects for life. The self-image with which a person felt at ease before the illness struck is not valid any more. For instance, the loss of an arm demands a new self-image because one element of the triad—physical, psychological, spiritual—has changed radically. The condition caused by the illness is unfamiliar to the patient. To incorporate this "unfamiliar" image into a new balance of physical, psychological, and spiritual wholeness with which the person feels at ease is a difficult task. Our culture and society focus strongly on performance and productivity. An incurable illness forms an obstacle to performance. In some cases the illness might even be paralyzing. The image by which a person lived and worked in the past has lost its validity. The individual is left in a state of uncertainty and doubt with regard to his or her own identity and value.

A person's response to God normally takes on the shape of the individual's response to life. One's personal value before God cannot be measured in terms of external success, but in the individual's mind there is a very close connection between accepting oneself and being acceptable to God, between being able to do things for God and to have value in God's eyes. When performance and productivity are lost, this radical change enters deeply into the person's relationship with God.

B. Loss of One's Identity

Identity may be described as "the recognition of a set of qualities and characteristics that make an individual thing or person what it, or he or she, is and make it distinct from any other thing or person." Such characteristics are often related to abilities or productivity. When these abilities cannot function anymore, a person can hardly recognize him or herself. There is a danger of losing one's identity, and with the loss of identity one's sense of self-value is seriously endangered. When the usual work-routine, professional position, and bread-winning responsibilities cannot be fulfilled, many people do not know what to do with themselves. Every person reacts in his or her own way. Some people can take such things in stride; others may be paralyzed in the same circumstances. The relationship with God usually follows the pattern of the human relationship to self and to others and will be affected by the loss of identity. It is hard to see personal importance when one cannot do or contribute anything. It is hard to see God's loving guidance when a serious illness brings pain and misery.

C. Fear of the Unknown

Fear of the unknown is a source of anxiety for almost all people, but it has a special meaning for patients with an incurable illness. A person who moves to a foreign country and culture will most likely experience apprehension, if not fear, because of the unfamiliarity with the language, new surroundings and new demands. Similarly, a person who starts a new job may experience apprehension until he or she gets used to the demands of the job in the current circumstances. But these persons can and do rely on their own abilities and previous experience. Through past experiences they know their strength and limitations. This knowledge gives a certain degree of self-confidence. Persons with incurable illness cannot rely on past experiences in the same way. Their "normal" way of acting and working can not be used any more. They have no experience of the demands that might possibly be made on them in the future. Such uncertainty can be for many people a frightening experience.

This fear of the unknown in incurable illness is also different from the fear of dying. Death is the great unknown, but everyone knows that our human capacities do not function after death. The incurably ill person's capacities do not cease to be operational when the illness strikes, but their operation is of a different and unknown nature. It is an uncertainty that demands to build up a new lifestyle in which the experience of brokenness needs to be transformed into a new personal wholeness which includes the brokenness as a part of its being.

The human response to God will go through similar developmental stages. When productivity was the main source for personal value, its disappearance will also affect the person's relationship to God. How often have we seen persons becoming embittered and unbearable after suffering a stroke or when they grow old. They never succeeded in incorporating their brokenness into an acceptable wholeness for their present existence.

The need to build up personal confidence and personal value for peace of mind is equally necessary with regard to God. It is important to understand the relationship between the physical and psychological condition of the patient, but not less important is the understanding of this relationship to the spiritual condition where the patient is at this time of his or her life.

II. *Psychological and spiritual needs in patients with certain incurable illnesses*

A. PATIENTS WITH CANCER

There are good reasons to argue that there do not exist "cancer patients" but that there are "patients with cancer." The main reason is that this directs the focus on the patient rather than on the disease. There are many different kinds and forms of cancer. Many of them are curable if they are detected early enough; others are not. Each patient reacts to it in a different way and handles it in a different way. One might say that there are as many different kinds of cancer as there are patients who suffer from it. But whatever the exact kind of cancer may be from which a person is suffering, it is a common reaction that cancer is perceived as a death sentence that is slowly executed. Despite its necessarily personal dimension, there are certain psychological and spiritual conditions that may be expected in such patients.

Depression

One of the first and most general reactions to the initial diagnosis of cancer is depression. Depression is a complex emotion, often combining fear, anger, loss of value, and frustration. The diagnosis of cancer may easily cause a sense of self-condemnation or accusation because the patient may feel somehow responsible for the illness through heavy smoking, unhealthy eating habits or otherwise. Consequently, the depression may be accompanied by a feeling of guilt.

Since cancer is so easily considered by the patient as a death sentence, the prospects of life are dim and expectations are lower. A feeling of inadequacy or of worthlessness may dominate the patient's attitude. Self-value and productivity are threatened. Fear takes control of the person. To the degree that self-value is seriously diminished, there is a growing expectation of rejection by others. It is a common human tendency to project one's own feelings onto others. The inability to accept oneself as a "person with cancer," or to maintain one's self-esteem and sense of personal value despite the illness, is likely to be projected on other people as if they will reject the patient as well. The "projected rejection by others" becomes an excuse for self-rejection. James who was in his late forties was diagnosed with incurable lung cancer. The usual out-going, hard-working and responsible breadwinner withdrew into his shell, did not want any visitors except his wife and children, and became totally absorbed in his own misery. It took a lot of patience to pull him out of this condition.

Inadequacy and fear of rejection create feelings of helplessness and hopelessness. These, in turn, increase the fear that all treatment will be ineffective. The sense of hopelessness easily slips into self-pity. The self-pitying patient may easily become lethargic and develop a self-defeating attitude that stands in the way of his or her own healing process[4] or of the process to find wholeness in their brokenness. This wholeness will include the cancer as an unavoidable part of being, but the patient experiences oneself as a person of full value and dignity despite one's limitations.

The psychological tendencies that affect a patient with cancer will also affect his or her spirituality or approach to God. Depression contains a degree of self-rejection and of anger against God or against the fact that cancer has struck. Initially the patient experiences self-doubt and self-rejection. However, a person who rejects oneself usually finds it very difficult to feel acceptable to God. Since the patient has developed a new and often negative perspective on life because of the incurable illness, it is necessary to develop a new vision on God as well. Serving God receives a new meaning because of the changed physical condition. Living with a different vision on life demands also living with God from the perspective of this new vision.

Stress

Stress is the response of the body to demands that are being put on it. Physical as well as emotional demands cause a strain and pressure that create a tension in the individual that affects

---

[4] *Psychological Treatment of Cancer Patients. A Cognitive, Behavioral Approach.* William Golden, Wayne Gersh, David Robbins, Allyn and Bacon (Boston, 1992) 10–15.

the body. The threshold of tolerance is different for every individual, but whatever the level of tolerance, stress plays a role in the process of coping with illnesses.

Cancer related stresses can have various sources. There can be fear of treatment, such as radiation, chemotherapy, or surgery. The fear of treatment often includes the fear of deformation as in mastectomy, the loss of hair, the discomfort of a colostomy, and other bodily discomforts. Another stressor, closely related to the fear of treatment, is the fear of dying, which, in most instances, is embodied in the fear of the pain, discomfort, and misery that proceeds death. The fear, guilt, or sadness of not being able to continue to care for one's loved ones is a stressor that applies to many serious illnesses, but it has a special meaning in patients with cancer. The incurability of the disease and the decrease of financial resources intended for the maintenance of the family often adds a new stress factor.

Living under stress has a strong influence on one's relationship with God. Stress takes away the inner peace; it urges to action, but it paralyzes when action is impossible. Fear also interferes with inner peace. It undermines security and trust and, consequently, the patient's trust in God needs to be reassessed and reformulated. One trusts in God in the way one is. In health a person looks at God from his or her perspective of health; in illness the perspective is from the point of illness and powerlessness. Cancer demands the development of a new spiritual perspective.

B. Patients with Acquired-Immuno-Deficiency-Syndrome (AIDS)

The following observations are intended to give some insights as how to provide pastoral support and guidance to patients suffering from AIDS. The medical aspects of AIDS are not part of these reflections. However, because of the very close relationship between physical, psychological and spiritual perspectives in human life, it is necessary to mention some of the physical and medical elements that are involved. Susan Folkman says: "The psychosocial effects of HIV disease cannot be understood without some knowledge of the disease itself."[5] The same is true with regard to the understanding of spiritual needs.

In today's literature we often find the expression HIV = Human Immunodeficiency Virus rather than the expression AIDS. AIDS is seen as the terminal result of the HIV infection.[6] AIDS itself is a *syndrome*, i.e., a conglomerate of diseases that are often unrelated to AIDS but that easily occur and become fatal because of the immunodeficiency in the patient.

AIDS is one of the most devastating illnesses a person can experience, not only because there is no cure for it but primarily for what it does to a person. Full-blown AIDS is not only physically devastating, but it has an exceptionally deep effect on the psyche as well. It affects the person's sense of self-value, the individual's relationship with family and friends, and consequently, also the relationship with God. I will focus on three aspects:

1. Physical characteristics of persons with AIDS.

2. Psychological and emotional needs that can be expected in persons with AIDS.

3. Spiritual needs that are common in persons with AIDS.

The recognition of the needs is the first step in the assessment of the patient's spirituality and the appropriate pastoral response.

1. Physical characteristics of persons with AIDS

AIDS is an Acquired Immunodeficiency Syndrome. Its basis and characteristic is the destruction of the individual's immune system. This will have little or no external symptoms as long

---

[5] Susan Folkman, "Psychosocial Effects of HIV Infection" in Leo Goldberger and Shlomo Breznitz *Handbook of Stress. Theoretical & Clinical Aspects* (New York: Free Press, 1993) 658.

[6] Walter Smith, S.J. "Embracing Pastoral Ministry in the Age of AIDS" in Robert Wicks and Richard Parsons, eds., *Clinical Handbook of Pastoral Counseling*, vol. 2 (New York: Paulist Press, 1993) 679.

as the person does not come in contact with any bacteria or virus which carry diseases. If such contact is established, the individual has no resistance and is open to any kind of opportunistic infection for which he or she has no longer a built-in protection or strength to overcome. While detailed study of physical symptoms of the disease is beyond the scope of this study, it is necessary to mention some basic physical and medical elements, because "The psycho-social effects of HIV disease cannot be understood without some knowledge of the disease itself."[7]

A) PHYSICAL AND MEDICAL ELEMENTS

AIDS is, in the first place, a disease of the immune system in the human body. The body has a built-in protection system in which special body-cells attack and, usually, eliminate invading viruses that would endanger the person's health. The bodily protection system consists, in a very broad outline, of three major cell-groups:

Phagocytes = scavenger cells that rid the body of foreign materials, dead tissue and degenerated cells;

Lymphocytes = white blood cells that patrol the body to alert for foreign invaders. They attack infected cells so that they cannot reproduce any further;

T-Cells = helper cells, are a form of lymphocytes that coordinate and manage the activities of the immune system.

The immuno-deficiency virus is extremely difficult to detect and can move in the body without being attacked by the protection system. The HIV (virus) invades the T-Cell and becomes part of its DNA so that it can reproduce itself with the help of the T-Cell. When these "helper-cells" are infected the whole immune system falls apart and the person becomes defenseless against the attack of any other kind of virus or bacteria.[8] Persons who have contracted HIV do not necessarily

[7] See note 5.
[8] Smith, 681–2.

have AIDS. AIDS means that they also have contracted some of the opportunistic infections for which they are now exceptionally susceptible.[9] A person can be HIV+ for many years and live a normal life. The so-called opportunistic infections (= infections that are unrelated to HIV but which have the free rein because of the break-down of the immune system) attack the person who now has no protection against them.

Because of its pernicious character, its mysterious nature and its many incurable forms, many metaphors and myths arose around AIDS. Some are more important for our discussion, such as:[10]

B) *AIDS as a homosexual illness*

Since AIDS was first discovered among homosexual males, it was largely considered as a homosexual disease. Modern research suggests that there are several strains of HIV. Some strains are more prominent among homosexual people while others occur more easily among heterosexuals, although neither strain is limited to any one category. The strain that is prominent in the United States occurs more easily, but by no means exclusively, among homosexual persons. As a consequence, HIV increased homophobia and harmed gay-rights movements. Because of its apparent homosexual connection, it also became a cause of rejection in many churches and religious communities. Thus it placed a severe stigma on all AIDS patients, even though it is now well established that women and heterosexuals can and do get infected with the immunodeficiency virus.

C) *AIDS as sex*

Because of its discovery among the homosexual community and its easy transmission through sexual relations, sex and sexual behavior have become locked-in with the concept of AIDS, despite the discovery that there are three primary paths of transmission: (1) sexual contact with an infected individual,

---

[9] John Bartlett and Ann K. Finkbeiner, eds., *The Guide to Living with HIV Infection* (Baltimore: Johns Hopkins University Press, 1994).

[10] Judith Landau-Stanton and Colleen Clements, *AIDS, Health and Mental Health. A Primary Resource Book* (New York: Brunner/Mazel, 1993) 4.

(2) exposure to infected blood or blood product, and (3) perinatal from an infected mother to her child.[11] AIDS is often, at least implicitly, seen as a result of illicit or immoral sexual behavior. This places a moral stigma on all AIDS sufferers, even though it is often undeserved.

D) *AIDS AS SELF-INFLICTED ILLNESS*

The opinion that AIDS is primarily caused by illicit or immoral sexual behavior makes AIDS easily understood as a self-inflicted and behaviorally-caused illness. This has a direct and negative psychological impact upon the patient. This impact has a social meaning, namely, the patient is personally responsible for the illness, as well as a spiritual meaning, such as, the patient is immoral or indecent and does not deserve to be a member of the worshipping community. The reasoning is something like this: self-chosen risk behavior, — self-accountability, — self-blame, — self-deserved illness, — need for moral instead of medical treatment, — non-deserving of medical or social resources.

As a consequence of this reasoning, there is often a lack of compassion in many communities and an increase of personal guilt in the patient. Although many more metaphors and myths do exist, these few will help the chaplain in his or her concern for the patients with HIV.

E) *A SYNDROME OF DISEASES*[12]

As mentioned earlier, AIDS is characterized by many diseases which find easy access to an individual and are often fatal because of the destruction of the immune system. Without trying to list them all, we may mention the following illnesses which are more prominent.

(PCP) Pneumocystis Carinii Pneumonia is a form of pneumonia caused by a yeast infection in the lungs. It is caused by a parasite that occurs in healthy animals and humans but which is fatal for the HIV+ person. The chances of recovery decrease

---

[11] Folkman, 658.
[12] Smith, 683.

with every attack of PCP. It is the most frequently occurring cause of death among AIDS patients.

(KS) Karposi's Sarcoma is a cancerous tumor of the cells lining blood and lymphatic vessels. It is usually not fatal in other persons but it increases the vulnerability of the HIV patient, particularly when the sarcoma occurs in the throat or internal organs.

(CMV) Cytomegalovirus and other viruses contribute to the inflammation and destruction of the retina, causing partial blindness. It also triggers seizures and dementia.

Taxoplasmosis attacks the central nervous system and causes brain seizures, high fevers and delirium, resulting in decreased levels of consciousness and triggering significant personality changes. It is treatable, but the treatment must be maintained for life.

Cryptosporidiosis Taxoplasmosis causes diarrhea that is sustained and life-threatening.

2. Psychological and emotional needs that can be expected in persons with AIDS.

Patients with AIDS may be considered a special category. Their emotional needs not only run very deep, but they are also varied and seem like tentacles that penetrate deep into the person, strangulate the individual's personality, and zap his or her energy. We need to remember that AIDS is the break-down of the immune system. With physical defenses broken down, the person becomes extremely vulnerable. There is little or nothing between the individual and any approaching disease or infection.

There is a great likelihood that the psychological condition follows the physical condition, so that also psychologically the human resistance has broken down or is extremely weakened. The physical vulnerability will be reflected in a psychological vulnerability as well. A little earlier I enumerated the major physical conditions and dangers we can expect in patients with AIDS. This fear for infection is not merely a physical danger, it includes very deep psychological stresses and emotions.

We need to look at these stresses and emotions that affect them as persons. Much of the following information is based upon Robert Perelli's study on *Ministry to Persons with AIDS*.[13] Perelli enumerates six major stress areas in the life of persons with AIDS: loss, anger, fear, guilt, shame and stigma, and secrecy. These stresses are closely interrelated.

The loss that is suffered by a person with AIDS is all encompassing. The major hardship is not the loss of health but the condition and consequences that directly follow from the disease.

a) *Loss of sexuality.* Loss of sexuality is not the loss of physical sexual functioning. Sexual functioning may stay intact for a long time. The disease touches much deeper and goes to the heart of being man or woman. The ability to relate to others on the deepest personal level has become a most likely way to transmit the disease to another person. Persons infected with the HIV virus will remain contagious for the rest of their lives and must indeed be considered to be a life-threatening danger in any form of physical human intimacy, even if no full blown AIDS has developed. Any form of romantic relationship is filled with danger and becomes an uneasy experience for the patient as well as for any partner. In addition to the physical danger, this contagious condition is attached to the personality of the patient and affects the individual's sense of personal value. The consequent possible loss of a lover or the fear in most people to establish any close relationship is a source for "imposed" isolation and deep loneliness.

b) *Loss of identity* occurs often in persons with AIDS and is a source of strong negative emotions. Almost invariably the disease leads to the loss of one's job. This, in turn, will take away the person's support for oneself and possibly for one's family. Job, position, ability to care for loved ones are usually closely related to a person's identity and self-image. Whatever sense of personal dignity and value existed in the individual is severely threatened by the disease that frequently includes

[13] Robert J. Perelli, *Ministry to Persons with AIDS. A Family Systems Approach* (Minneapolis: Augsburg, 1991) 29–40.

shame and guilt. Shame can be expected because of the stigma that society places on persons with AIDS.

Guilt occupies a special place in the feelings of persons with AIDS and provides the feeding ground for shame and stigma. Guilt is usually difficult to counteract because it often touches the deepest layers of the personality. Reassuring statements such as "It was not your fault" or "You cannot change the past" are rarely effective. With Barlett and Finkbeiner[14] I agree that "Guilt, except when it keeps you from repeating mistakes, is a remarkably useless emotion." However, this gives little consolation unless one can tackle the source or nature of guilt and turn the experience of guilt into a source of positive energy. To achieve this goal we need to distinguish between psychological guilt and moral guilt.

Psychological guilt is the negative, self-rejecting feeling about oneself for which one cannot indicate any valid reason. It seems to be a tendency that is inherent to the personality, telling the individual that he or she is not and will never be the whole and worthwhile individual that one is expected to be. It gives a constant awareness of an insufficiency for which one is somehow personally to be blamed, even though one is not aware of any wrongdoing. It is the underlying tendency toward self-rejection that was present even before any diagnosis of HIV+ but that after the diagnosis returns with increased vigor and paralyzes the patient. The only cure for this condition is a continued personal experience of being a person of value and being acceptable. This is a slow and difficult process that demands much patience on the part of the care-giver.

Moral guilt is a similar negative and self-rejecting feeling, but in this case the cause of the feeling can be traced back to failures in personal behavior, in human relationships or social unfairness for which the individual perceives, rightly or wrongly, a personal responsibility. Moral guilt is something that results from a personal involvement which one wants to undo. It is a deficiency that the person has brought on to oneself and that weighs him or her down before God and neighbor. The individual is personally responsible for this deficiency, but once steps

[14] Barlett and Finkbeiner, 95.

have been taken toward restoration or repair, the sense of being personally rejectable disappears. Moral guilt is attached to responsible activity; psychological guilt is attached to the person.

Guilt is often connected with AIDS because the transmission of the disease may have resulted from a form of behavior that society finds reprehensible, such as the use of drugs or homosexual relationships. There is literally nothing of their past healthy condition that remains as a support for the infected guilt-ridden person. The statement that God is forgiving and merciful or that the neighbor has accepted his or her apologies, is usually insufficient. He or she needs to give a personal proof of change of behavior before inner peace can be fully restored. The cure lies in guiding the person through the acknowledgement of the reason for guilt and the readiness to take the steps to do whatever can be done at this moment to prove that he or she has changed in mentality and approach to life. Here again the care-giver is faced with a delicate process that demands a very high degree of patience, understanding and compassion.

c) *Loss of control over life.* When the immune system has become largely or totally inoperative, the individual is defenseless against all attacks of disease or infection. The only protection a person has left is avoidance, but most people are not sure what to avoid or what may pose a danger for infection. This leaves the patient with a deep sense of personal insecurity. Although this insecurity may primarily refer to the physical condition, it will also affect the emotional and spiritual condition of the patient.

d) *Loss of meaning and hope.* A large segment of the meaning of life is based upon professional activity and relationships, where prospects for the future give hope and courage. All this disappears in persons with AIDS. In most cases they have lost self-respect, and because of this self-rejection they feel that they have also lost and do not deserve the respect that others used to give them. The loss of meaning and hope for life makes it difficult to establish any meaningful relationship with care-givers or counselors or to develop a basis for rebuilding the personality. Care-givers and counselors must prove that they indeed care as persons. Their function or profession is no guarantee. Yet any rebuilding must be based upon personal value and dignity.

Pastoral Implications

The above brief observations suggest some consequences for the pastoral concern for patients with HIV:

a. *They suffer under a stigma* of being homosexual and of illicit sexual behavior. This stigma has both social and religious implications.

b. *They feel rejected by their own family and church* so that almost all of their support systems are removed.

c. *They often experience a sense of worthlessness* as a consequence of their socially unacceptable illness.

d. *They often experience a sense of personal guilt* even when the disease is not caused by any form of ill behavior.

e. *They experience anger* against society and against their religious denomination for having rejected them, at least in the patient's opinion.

f. *They experience anger against God* for allowing them to suffer from this illness.

g. *They experience a need for God and religious values.* Their experience of helplessness urges them to reach out to another power over their life. Even though they feel rejected by their own church, they still seek reconciliation with God, and often reconciliation with their own church-community.

These and many other needs will play a role in the concern and care of patients with HIV. In our pastoral approach we must always keep in mind the high level of vulnerability in the patient and their deep sense of powerlessness and defenselessness.

The three factors mentioned earlier (self-acceptance, meaningfulness to family and friends, and partnership with God) are indispensable for any building or rebuilding of any personality, but they are even more important for persons with AIDS. Fear, guilt, shame, and stigma are very severe handicaps for self-acceptance and for the sense of acceptability by others. The sense of guilt is not taken away by a statement that mistakes can be forgiven and that God is merciful. If there is guilt, they experience their illness as an irremovable result of their mistake. Their illness is a constant reminder and reality of their guilt. While the illness is present, the mistake remains, and with the illness also a sense of shame and stigma stays with them. What has been harmed or destroyed through interhuman experience needs another interhuman experience to be restored.

Rebuilding this self-acceptance in persons with AIDS is a slow process. Due to earlier experiences they will be inclined to test the sincerity and perseverance of the minister. This testing can take many different shapes from expressed doubt to apparent rejection. Kindness, understanding, and perseverance on the part of the minister are the only solution. Understanding often must include the acceptance, if not approval, of their way of life, be it homosexual, drug addiction, or any other form.

It may be said that once self-acceptance emerges, the relationships with family, friends and God will follow easily. Usually, however, there needs to be a simultaneous interaction between these three factors, so that the minister needs to work on all levels simultaneously.

Anger,[15] an inner discontent with a current situation and a defense mechanism against self-rejection, is closely related to the process of seeking an inner balance and self-acceptance. Anger may be directed against anyone and anything; however, anger against God most likely enters into it, since, in their view, God either caused their disease, did not prevent it or at least allowed it. This anger is aggravated by laws and customs of many church communities. Even if some individual churches and ministers show great acceptance and kindness, many official church authorities reject homosexual behavior

---

[15] For the HIV effects on emotions, see Bartlett and Finkbeiner, chapter 4, especially 79–95.

and with it people suffering from AIDS. To accept homosexual tendencies in a person but to reject their behavior is for many persons a contradiction or dishonesty. In many cases it may be necessary to help people to understand that one, as minister, can disagree with a certain behavior without necessarily condemning the individual.

Secrecy is a defense mechanism to protect oneself against rejection by family and friends. The fear of rejection already creates an emotional distance that inhibits self-acceptance and acceptance by family and friends. The fear of open rejection may be realistic. In such cases the minister has the delicate task of balancing honesty and confidentiality. One of the necessary approaches is to find out the deeper reason for secrecy.

These reasons may be found in many places, especially in the work place because the disease destroys job and life-security. Stigma and shame may contribute to the desire for secrecy. Sometimes the patient may feel that professional relationships and friendships, which are maintained despite the disease, may be considered a betrayal on his or her part because of the danger that they may transmit the disease.

Another reason for secrecy may be found in the family background. The patient may fear rejection on account of real or perceived family expectations. The family has to face illness, dependency, and death at an age "that should not have to deal with such problems." The illness disrupts the family plans and dreams. Religious orientations may consider AIDS a divine punishment. The family joins in executing this punishment by rejecting the patient. This fear or attitude offers another reason for secrecy.

In this whole adaptation process is a strong intermingling of personal, societal and religious elements which prevent the development of the three aspects required for internal peace and spiritual growth. Because of the many forms of rejection, self-acceptance becomes very difficult. The first step for the chaplain will be to show that he or she accepts the patient as a person. In a sense, the chaplain must prove him or herself as an accepting person. The chaplain, who is perceived as a religious and moral person, may count on it that he or she is in advance classified among the "non-accepting" individuals. Only deliberate accepting behavior, such as a hug or embrace, can change this.

In many instances the personal meaningfulness for family and friends, which is closely related to self-acceptance, needs a lot of attention. This meaningfulness is a very important factor for the patient. To a large degree, it decides whether the person has something or someone to live for or not and, consequently, it may indicate whether the patient finds life worth living.

Meaningfulness is also determined by the expectations of the family, by their dreams and hopes, as well as by their ability to accept changing conditions. The patient's place in the family before the illness is another major factor in meaningfulness for family and friends. Particularly if the patient was close to the rest of the family, the present separation can be painful. The closeness that could be the greatest support for self-value can become a major source of self-rejection. The patient's feelings may vary from painful sadness to anger, depending on the attitudes which he or she expects in the family. If there was no closeness, there is even more chance that anger will prevail. In any case, a new relationship is necessary before the person with AIDS can find peace with him or herself.

The third factor for inner peace and spiritual growth is the experience of a partnership with God. Such a partnership is hardly possible without self-acceptance and personal meaningfulness with people who are important in the patient's life. It will be very difficult, perhaps not even possible, to restore any of these three elements—acceptance, meaningfulness, and partnership—separately from each other. They are so interconnected that the growth in one aspect demands and contributes to the growth of the others. The vision on human wholeness, which changes so radically because of the illness, must always form the center and foundation of any pastoral approach and must be conveyed to the patient.

3. Spiritual needs that can be expected in AIDS patients.

Three elements lie at the heart of any form of spiritual life, namely,

a) the ability to see oneself as a person of value even without one's usual external involvement or success,

b) to relate to relatives and friends as if it were natural to count on them in circumstances in which one cannot help oneself anymore, and

c) to understand God as a partner in one's life who is present on the good days in which one can reach out to others for support as well as on the hard days when one has to acknowledge total dependence.

These three factors (self-acceptance, meaningfulness to family and friends, and partnership with God) form the heart of all forms of spiritual life, and therefore, they are the heart of the recognition of the spiritual needs in patients as well. I have stated this earlier in the definition of spirituality, namely, that spirituality is the personal attitude and behavior with which an individual responds to God. This personal attitude and behavior disclose the degree of the individual's self-respect and self-value. This self-respect and self-value is translated into the relationships toward family and community. It is also the basis on which the human relationship to God and to the religious community is built. We have seen in the previous section that these are precisely the psychological qualities where persons with AIDS are most seriously wounded. A reflection on the sources of personal and spiritual relationships which I have shown earlier can provide a framework for the understanding of their spiritual needs.

On page 25 we probed deeply into the quality, degree, and origin of the individual's self-image, and the experience of this image within the immediate human community. It tries to establish whether the personal and community value is positive or negative, to what degree, and why. To aid in these probings, the statements of sections two and three of the assessment instrument (pp. 25–29) provide a helpful guideline. Insight into these matters is not gained by letting the patient answer questions but rather by having a framework in one's mind which gives direction to the conversation.

On page 31 the probing is concerned about the patient's attitude, relations, and expectations with regard to God, the religious community or church, and the way in which he or she approaches God. This multiple perspective cannot be properly evaluated without taking into consideration the total person that exists as an individual and in the community. This total person responds to God according to his or her personal characteristics.

Helpful directives can be found in numbers 1, 4 and 5 of the assessment instrument. Trust and respect for God will necessarily take the form of the human ability to trust that exists in the individual. This individual form is also the point from which the chaplain can start to journey with the patient.

It is obviously impossible to discuss all imaginable forms and shades of interhuman and religious relationships. Let me venture to present two extremes of attitude and behavior which are imaginary but not far out, and leave it to the reader to see the shade between the extremes in which his or her patient may be.

John is a twenty-five-year-old man who was born into a very strict, controlling family. All the children were expected to observe minutely every rule of church, society and family, and to live up to the expectations of controlling parents. Transgressions were punished, and personal acceptance depended largely on the degree of obedience and the success in productivity. In addition, John was a homosexual, a condition which was strongly rejected by church and family. Due to strained family relationships John left home, took a job as a mechanic, lived his life as a homosexual, and was involved with drugs. The family heard about this and closed the door completely. John contracted AIDS. The family made it clear that this was his own fault and responsibility because of the life he was living.

We may expect that John's self-esteem is as low as can be imagined and that his reliance on family, church, and community was equally low. The imposition of prayer at home had turned him off, he was rejected by the church, and his homosexual relations that he felt he could not break placed him in a constant tension of irresistible attraction and deep feelings of guilt.

What John needs is to be accepted as a person for his own personal value. This acceptance must be experienced. The reassurance that God accepts all people makes no sense after the church or community has rejected him. The chaplain needs to combine within him or herself all these factors: personal acceptance, acceptance by the community of the church, whom the chaplain represents, and acceptance by God, since the chaplain comes to bring God's love. Any sign of personal hesitancy or distance on the part of the chaplain will enforce the negative experiences of the past. An intelligent, sensitive, and open-minded spiritual assessment combined with personal courage and generosity can provide the necessary pastoral guidance.

At the other extreme there is Terri, a dedicated housewife and mother in her mid-thirties. She came from a well-to-do believing family with an open mind to the changes in value expressed in today's society. With her husband and children she formed a loving family where mutual respect and trust were the primary characteristics. Through a blood transfusion she contracted AIDS. Her whole life and future fell to pieces.

In these circumstances she never lost the love and respect of her family. She remained respected and loved by husband, children, and parents. She maintained contact with her church and experienced continued support from her community.

There is no doubt that Terri's ordeal was extremely painful and difficult to deal with. However, her self-image was shaken but not broken. Her trust in God had to find a new basis since she could no longer offer what she used to offer. Her contribution to her church and community became totally different. But in all this her self-respect, her love for family and neighbor, and her devotion to God were not broken. The basis for personal, communal, and religious acceptance was still there and provided a basis for personal and spiritual growth. The chaplain or spiritual guide must start the journey at the point where the patient is by strengthening what is there and rebuilding what has been damaged.

These two examples are imaginary but not far-out. They give a perspective of a wide range of spiritual needs. They may help us to see how assessment can help in the pastoral responsibilities of a chaplain and other spiritual guides. They also may help to see that the assessment instrument is not a questionnaire through which we can draw a graph of where on a scale a patient is. Rather the instrument is a framework that assists the chaplain or spiritual leader to understand the patient and to be better able to provide that kind of support that deepens the patient's relationship with God. What this means for pastoral response and pastoral planning is the subject of the next chapter.

C. PATIENTS WITH MULTIPLE SCLEROSIS AND WITH AMYOTROPHIC LATERAL SCLEROSIS

Multiple sclerosis (MS) and amyotrophic lateral sclerosis (ALS) are both diseases of the central nervous system, but since they are different diseases with a different impact upon the physical, psychological and spiritual powers of the individual, they will be discussed individually.

1. Multiple sclerosis.[16]

MS is a disease in which parts of the protective covering (myelin sheath) of nerve tracts in the brain or in the spinal cord are inflamed or swollen. As a consequence nutrients are not properly fed to the nerves and electrical impulses do not pass through as is required. This disease can occur in the brain or in the spinal cord and will affect and disable the function that is served by that part of the brain or spinal cord.

Particularly in the early stages, the disease comes and goes and during the early remission periods the patient can function normally. There is no pattern in the recurrence of the attacks, but usually they become more frequent and more severe when the disease has been present for a longer period of time. In the later stages the patient may become seriously disabled, including walking, seeing, speaking, bladder control, etc. No effective medication has been found yet to combat the illness.

---

[16] Jeffrey R.M. Kunz and Asher J. Finkel, eds., *The AMA Family Medical Guide* (New York: Random House, 1987) 294. Charles Clayman, ed., *The AMA Home Medical Encyclopedia* (New York: Random House, 1989) 701.

The disease strikes approximately one out of every thousand persons. Two out of every three patients are women. It is debated whether the disease has a genetic basis.

The disease carries with it disabilities which cannot be cured and grow progressively worse. This has a serious psychological impact upon the patient. The disease-related physical disability affects self-confidence, self-esteem, and sense of value for oneself and for society. In certain circumstances, when the disease includes incontinence, it may also cause a sense of personal shame. For pastoral responses it is important to keep in mind (1) the incurability of the disease, (2) the psychological effects that accompany the illness, and (3) the functions that are weakened or destroyed by the disease.

2. Amyotrophic lateral sclerosis.[17]

ALS is the most often occurring of the diseases of the motor neuron system. It is a disease in which the nerves that control the muscular activities degenerate and die. The result is weakness and atrophy of the muscles. It occurs in about one in every hundred thousand people in the United States. There is no known cure. Every part of the body can be affected (lungs, throat, extremities, etc.). Affected parts of the body slowly stop functioning, and this paralysis can lead to a slow and painful death.

Psychological and spiritual consequences are largely the same as in multiple sclerosis, involving self-esteem, self-confidence, self-value, etc. Understanding and patience are primary factors in pastoral care. All the physical circumstances of the patient's life undermine self-confidence and self-esteem. Encouragement will be gained not so much by reference to God's acceptance of our limitations as by building the conviction of "partnership with God." This partnership helps the patient to see the presence of God in the pain and frustrations as well as in the successes of self-expression. When physical abilities disintegrate, psychological and spiritual condition can unfold when patient and God form one principle of operation.

---

[17] *AMA Family Medical Guide,* 295, and *AMA Home Medical Encyclopedia,* 696.

D. PATIENTS WITH A SERIOUS PHYSICAL HANDICAP

This group is extremely broad and can include almost any form of prolonged physical discomfort or disability. Every handicap, illness, or chronic condition has its own nature with its own physical, psychological, and spiritual consequences. The serious physical handicap group, however, falls into a special category since the lives of the patients are not endangered in any way. They may be physically quite healthy, yet their handicap makes them different from other people since what other people take for granted is frequently beyond their reach. Such a situation can be very painful and, for some people, very difficult to handle.

Every physical handicap has its own concomitant psychological and spiritual demands. Such demands depend largely on (1) the nature of the handicap, (2) the place of the disabled function in the life of the patient, and (3) the patient's personal history and ability to cope with limitations.

Physical handicaps can be divided into broad categories of:

Passing handicaps that can be cured through medical treatment or in the course of time through more or less vigorous physical exercise that brings the function back to near or complete normality. This may include joint-replacements and even artificial limbs.

Permanent handicaps with which a person will have to live for the rest of his of her life. In this category we may find paralysis of any kind, loss of irreplaceable limbs, speech defect, colostomy, etc.

A common characteristic of such conditions is that the patients experience a loss of self-value, self-esteem, self-confidence, and other personal qualities. These losses are particularly important when the handicap touches on certain functions in which the patient used to find his or her personal value. The speed-skater is faced with a serious change of life when he or she loses a leg; for a carpenter the loss of a hand may be difficult to handle; for a musician the loss of hearing and for a painter the loss of sight may provide almost insurmountable obstacles to their usual and preferred self-expression. Such handicaps form a serious hardship for anyone in such circumstances, but they become particularly serious when such persons have placed their life value and fulfillment primarily in the activation of these functions or capacities. This means when personality and speed-skating, personality and wood-working, etc., coincide.

According to the circumstances it will be necessary to (1) support and encourage the patient to regain one's abilities, or (2) help the patient to rebuild one's personality on a different value-basis than before. I will never forget the privilege I once had to preside at the marriage ceremony of a young paraplegic, who had broken his neck in a diving accident, and a healthy young woman.

All throughout the marriage preparation, the signing of the papers, the religious ceremony, and the bridal dance at the reception, we all had to take him as a person of full human value in his own right. Through this constant experience of acceptance one could almost see the person grow in self-acceptance and spiritual depth.

The spiritual understanding of life and approach to life are closely related to self-acceptance and play a significant role in this process of rebuilding the personality. Vice versa, self-acceptance is strongly supported by the spiritual depth of the individual. Instances like this made me realize more than any other experience that ordinary human relationships can become a true exercise of ministry.

4

Pastoral Response and Pastoral Planning

The previous chapters show that any spiritual assessment must include the whole person. It is not enough to look only at the religious feelings of a person. It is necessary to assess the orientation of the person's life. A similar approach is necessary for a pastoral response. A truly pastoral response is usually different from spiritual encouragement or pious statements. "Pastoral" means the guidance of the total person toward the manifestation of God's love and goodness. Pastoral guidance or a pastoral response must take the patient's physical and psychological condition very seriously. Spirituality is not an added quality that is to be superimposed upon a perfect personality or that is added to an existing personality. It is rather the perspective that gives meaning and direction to the attitudes and self-realization of the individual.

For instance, James, a highly qualified heavy-equipment operator, lost his left arm in an accident. Physically he healed perfectly. Rehabilitation and job retraining enabled him to work most effectively with smaller equipment. In his own mind, however, he remained the handicapped and mutilated heavy-equipment operator. He was angry with God, and he took his anger out on his wife and children and on his pastor. His attitudes and behavior suggest an understanding of God as a caretaker who is derelict in his duties to protect and guide people like James. To be pastoral with James one cannot simply advise him to accept his condition. Pastoral concern will assist James to find value in himself as a person with one arm who responds to God in a new way.

Once a chaplain is acquainted with the possible psychological and spiritual needs of persons with incurable diseases, he or she needs to formulate a response that offers the individual support and guidance to live with his or her condition. On purpose I do not say to cope with his or her condition, but rather to live with it. To cope means to me that the situation is never integrated into the personality. The patient keeps "fighting" his or her condition and is involved in a struggle that cannot be won. This fight will never give satisfaction. There will never be an inner peace. To live with an incurable condition reflects for me the ability to integrate one's condition into one's life and to learn to be at peace with this unwanted but unavoidable reality. This is no fatalism. Such a person will make every effort to minimize the consequences of the disease, to heal as far as possible and to make life livable. Whatever strength and abilities are still operative will be activated. Such a person will live his or her life to the fullness that can be achieved at this moment and maintain a personal value and dignity. Such a person can experience personal wholeness in the condition of brokenness.

I. *Pastoral response and pastoral planning for patients with incurable illnesses*

Any pastoral response needs to include and to be based upon a response to the needs that are common to persons with incurable illnesses in general. These common traits, however, are modified and focused by the needs that are characteristic of particular diseases.

The patient who wants to learn to live with any incurable illness such as cancer, AIDS, Multiple Sclerosis or a serious handicap needs to have or to develop:

> 1. *A positive self-concept* that may incorporate professionalism and productivity, but that is not identifiable with either of these two concepts.

2. *An honest understanding of the strengths and weaknesses* of his or her personal and professional abilities in the light of the incurable condition he or she has.

3. *An honest understanding of the illness* with its debilitating qualities and a realistic view of the prognosis.

4. *An understanding of the basic motivation of his or her life* and how this motivation can stimulate one's abilities within the limits that the illness imposes.

These four qualities or characteristics allow patients to see themselves in a true and realistic light. They are no longer controlled by dreams of returning to past abilities and successes. The past may be an encouraging and pleasant memory which can contribute to their self-esteem. It may give satisfaction to remember the strength they once had, but it is not the standard at which they look as an ideal for the present. Once these characteristics are in place, a new growth process becomes possible which can lead to a new and possibly original self-expression. If a chaplain wants to play a role in this process, he or she must assess the patient on these terms and map the road that can lead to corresponding results. Spiritual assessment becomes a major tool in this task.

When working with patients with incurable diseases, the chaplain needs to blend three perspectives into one approach:

a) *the assessment*—what is the psychological and spiritual condition of this person,

b) *the pastoral response*—what appropriate sign of understanding and encouragement can be offered to this person,

c) *the pastoral planning*—by which steps can this person be guided to integrate his or her condition into everyday life, or to maintain or deepen this integration.

Although there are similarities between various illnesses, each illness deserves its own separate reflection.

A. Persons with Incurable Cancer

The Assessment

Throughout contact with the patient, the chaplain has continually assessed the patient's personal and spiritual condition. The chaplain has discovered to what degree the characteristic, such as depression, stress, or fear, controls or is controlled by the patient with cancer. The chaplain may also have an insight about which underlying personality trait shapes the kind of depression or fear that the patient experiences. It is then his or her task to offer appropriate guidance by assisting the patient to handle and integrate their painful condition.

Look again at James whom we met on page 48. He withdrew completely into his shell. He had built up his business from scratch, and now, at age forty-nine, he looked forward to giving to his wife and children a comfortable life and bright future. This all fell to pieces. His task was not yet completed. He failed. To add to the misery, he had been a heavy smoker against the advice of his wife and children. The sense of failure and guilt made him withdraw. He was angry with life and was ashamed to see friends and neighbors who could only pity him.

With the help of his wife and children the chaplain could discuss with James the involvement in building the business, the energy and pride connected with it. Slowly we could begin to discuss how this could continue and develop further, even when he was not there. From leadership in the business, he could step back to be the major advisor. A sense of personal dignity and value returned and an inner peace allowed him to find happiness in his relationship with family and with God.

The Pastoral Response

The purpose of a pastoral response is to assist the patient to find an inner peace through acceptance of self and of one's condition from the perspective of one's ultimate value and goal in life (God). Inner peace is not achieved by covering up but by developing one's sense of dignity as a person. This dignity is not destroyed, not even violated, by a physical disease. A disease may threaten our life and eventually kill us, but it needs not to destroy our human dignity. Human dignity is expressed in the ability to integrate the condition in which we find ourselves into an achievement of wholeness through a balance of the physical, psychological and spiritual dimensions of our lives. James managed to integrate his incurable cancer into his present life. He found a new goal in life: to enable his wife and children to continue. In this new sense of wholeness, he found peace with himself and with God.

A pastoral response does not start with the assurance that God cares. The idea of a caring God is meaningless for a patient whose personal identity is almost totally contained in being a professional, a spouse or a parent. This personal identity may seem completely ruined by unbearable and incurable cancer.

A response becomes pastoral when the reality of the patient's condition is acknowledged with all its hardship, frustration and inner desperation. Empathy and "being with the patient" in whatever condition he or she might be, whether this condition be a flaming rage, a numb defeat, or an effort to active integration, may sometimes be the only valid pastoral response. Obviously the chaplain cannot leave the patient there indefinitely. He or she needs to initiate a process of transition and growth. The immediate response, however, is very important. It may set the tone for further pastoral care.

The Pastoral Planning

The goal of pastoral care is "that the patient find inner peace with oneself, with the surrounding world and with God." This goal may never be far from the chaplain's mind. The chaplain, however, needs to evaluate and prioritize the obstacles that stand in the way of inner peace. In the final analysis, inner peace is God's gift. Hence the temptation is to draw God into the picture as soon as possible. We may not overlook that God usually does not work independently from the person but guides and stimulates each one proportionate to his or her personal investment and search. Consequently, the chaplain's approach needs to focus on the perspective that the patient is called to be one principle of operation with God. Every effort to gain self-esteem and self-confidence brings the patient one step closer to peace in a collaborative openness to God's presence.

A pastoral treatment plan must be flexible. The patient's condition and attitude is subject to many changes, and roads toward progress have many ups and downs. The important factor is that the minister develop a plan of action. Such plan of action is best established in cooperation with the patient. Ultimately, it is his or her life and happiness that is at stake. A patient can come to the insight that the condition is incurable and that the only way to find peace is to integrate rather than deny or fight it. This means to accept oneself as a person with whom cancer is inseparably connected but who can live his or her life to its fullness despite the cancer rather than being a person who spends all his or her energy in fighting against it. The patient will then also experience that "living life to its fullness" in the present circumstances is the most effective way to fight against the illness. Such integration is possible. It does not mean fatalism but an active self-realization of one's qualities as far as possible at this time. Integration means working at one's fullest capacity toward the wholeness of one's being. In this search for wholeness, God's grace and God's presence blend with the patient's efforts to create a peace and acceptance that form a wholeness of personal surrender to God.

B. Patients with Acquired-Immune-Deficiency-Syndrome

Persons with AIDS form a special category because of its enormous and devastating impact upon the individual and upon his or her surroundings. Their care demands more space in our discussion.

The Assessment

In our pastoral concern some major characteristics concerning AIDS need to be kept in mind because they color every self-image and they give a special flavor to every pastoral approach.

1. AIDS has no known cure.

2. In its advanced forms it is physically devastating and through opportunistic infections it can cause much pain and misery.

3. Certain forms of infection may cause mental deficiency.

4. It has a severe stigma attached to it.

The stigma which is attached to AIDS is the basis for a feeling and perhaps even for an experience of rejection by family and community, including one's church-community. The rejection touches the deepest layers of the personality. It touches the patient's capacity for intimacy. If the patient contracted the virus through previous sexual relations, there may be a sense of guilt or stigma. In any case, for such persons any sexual contact would mean a serious danger for the partner. This loss of the ability for full intimacy touches the heart of one's personal value and of being man or woman.

Rejection is always painful, perhaps especially for persons with AIDS. The resentment for being rejected easily causes a deep anger which directs itself against individuals and society, often against their religious society. Because of this rejection, many persons with AIDS develop a paranoia against people in general and against people in the helping profession in particular. A minister often must prove him or herself before he or she can offer any effective ministry.

The identity crisis in persons with AIDS is of a special kind and more severe than in other illnesses. There is a stigma that destroys one's confidence in one's manhood or womanhood; there is the rejection, perceived or real, by the civil and religious community; there is the inability to work one's job at a time when one should be at the height of productivity. Everything connected with personal development and human relationships has come to a screeching halt and seems to be cut off. The surroundings in which persons with AIDS live is often not conducive to restore or build relationships, and, even if the surroundings were conducive to growth, the personal anger often proves a serious obstacle for the development of any form of new relationships.

The patient's weaknesses are evident, and their strengths are often hard to find because of the deep personal and professional destruction that has taken place. Few people understand the illness and fewer still can predict its course because of the many different opportunistic infections that can develop. The uncertainty contributes to isolation and anger. There is hardly any other disease that destroys so effectively human relationships and hopes.

The motivation to search for a personal wholeness is usually very low, and the parameters of the illness within which a patient can look for any form of self-realization are very limited. There are very few "natural" support systems left to build upon. Without being overly pessimistic, an assessment of the patient is likely to offer an enormous challenge for appropriate and effective pastoral care. The chaplain needs to be alert to what is going on in the patient. The patient's view of self, life, and relationships during this time of illness sets the tone for his or her attitude and contribution to wholeness.

At this point look at John and Terri whom we met earlier. John's view of self has a totally different quality than Terri's. John must experience acceptance from the lowest possible level. He has no support groups upon which he can fall back. His religious value system is unbelievably weak. Terri has a solid basis. She has human support systems, and she has faith.

The patient's past experiences are another important aspect. If there have been earlier illnesses or painful struggles that have been successfully handled, there may be a personal strength that will enable the patient to deal with the present situation. We can expect this to be present in Terri who, as wife and mother, has faced and overcome many difficult situations. If he or she did not have such earlier experiences, as in John's case, then the present condition may be a novel and extra burden. Age and professional or family responsibilities may play a role in increasing depression or stress.

Equally important is the patient's understanding of the illness. Is he or she aware of how incurable the disease is or how debilitating it can become? Based upon his or her degree of knowledge, the patient has built up a corresponding personal attitude and self-image that can deal with the situation. From this knowledge the patient's expectations can be assessed, whether they are denials or a realistic view of his or her condition. Some people need to deny their condition in order to be able to face life. To help them reach beyond denial into reality is extremely difficult and painful. Realism is considerably more likely to deal effectively with the progressive nature of the disease than pessimism or denial.

The patient's expectations and hopes will also tell the story about the underlying motivation. Realism fosters positive and constructive contributions. Denials, although they may sometimes be necessary to protect the person, do not lend themselves to the creation of wholeness and inner peace.

The insight into all these areas describe the person who is suffering and who needs support. Each of the statements that detail the five categories of the Assessment Instrument plays a role. The person with AIDS has a self-image that is highlighted in the evaluation of statements a, b, c, and d of category 2, which speaks about the positive or negative degree of self-pity or self-rejection (see pp. 26–27), about the presence or absence of anger, acceptability or inner peace. The statements of categories 3 and 4 assess the intensity or the degree of the person's relationship with and trust in the civil and religious community to which the person belongs and from which he or she expects or does not expect support and understanding.

Categories 5 and 1 show what place God and prayer may play in the person's life, in particular under the pressure of the illness.

All these categories and statements interlock. The degree of self-esteem and the understanding of God as either a source of personal and loving strength or as a punitive judge will be very closely related. The feeling of rejection and of anger toward the community are tied together. The feeling of self-acceptance and trust in the community form one general category. Personal guilt, anger toward the community, and the feeling of being rejected by God go hand in hand, while, if acceptance and forgiveness are experienced in the community, trust in God's forgiveness and love can much more easily develop and, in turn, strengthen the human relationships.

The strong interlocking that comes to the surface in these few examples shows the importance of understanding the interactive nature of spirituality described in chapter 1. The chaplain must formulate in his or her own mind the appropriate pastoral response.

The Pastoral Response

Any pastoral response must be based upon the reality of life and must view life as it is in its interhuman relationship and in its relationship to God. AIDS is no exception. Where the trust in humanity has severely suffered because of perceived or real rejection by individuals and community, regaining trust will be of the highest priority. Rebuilding trust presupposes an appropriate involvement of physical (contact), emotional (understanding, empathy, and respect), and spiritual acceptance.

The absence of almost all external physical support systems can sometimes pave the way for a reliance upon spiritual values and qualities. However, the rejection by the religious community or congregation makes the establishment of a spiritual trust more difficult. A pastoral response must carefully search for the proper balance. To achieve such a balance demands wise pastoral planning and must take into consideration that no one except the individual patient him or herself can establish this balance.

Let me repeat what I stated earlier. The purpose of a pastoral response is to assist the patient in finding an inner peace through acceptance of self and of one's condition from the perspective of one's ultimate value and goal in life (which is God). Inner peace is not achieved by covering up, but by developing one's sense of dignity as a person. This dignity is not necessarily destroyed or even violated by a physical disease. A disease may threaten one's life and eventually kill a person, but it need not destroy human dignity. Human dignity lies in the ability to integrate the condition in which one finds oneself into the experience of wholeness through the balance of the physical, psychological and spiritual dimensions of one's life.

A pastoral response does not start with the assurance that God cares. The idea of a caring God is meaningless to a patient whose personal identity as a professional, as spouse and parent seems completely ruined by the experience of an HIV-related infection. A response becomes pastoral when the reality of the patient's condition is acknowledged with all its hardship, frustration and inner desperation. Empathy and "being with the patient" in whatever condition he or she might be, whether this condition be a flaming rage, a numb defeat, or an effort toward active integration, could be the only valid pastoral response. Obviously the chaplain cannot support the patient indefinitely just by empathic presence. The care-giver needs to initiate a process of transition and growth. The immediate response, however, is very important. It may set the tone for further pastoral care.

Empathic listening is the first step in conveying to a person with AIDS a sense of personal value. Where guilt and an experience of rejection have caused self-rejection, anger, bitterness, and mistrust, empathic listening conveys acceptance, value, and respect as the building blocks for a new and healthy relationship. The experience of personal acceptance can lead to mutual acceptance and, in turn, to an accepting relationship between the individual and God. There is perhaps no form of pastoral care that needs to be built more strongly upon human relationships than the pastoral care of persons with AIDS for the simple reason that perhaps no disease distorts and upsets the personality more than AIDS. The spiritual care of persons with AIDS teaches us how much the human element is necessary for the expression of spiritual values, and how much *human wholeness* (the integration of physical, psychological, and spiritual values) is a requirement in the human service of God. A pastoral response must start with the acknowledgement of what can be seen and experienced.

The Pastoral Planning

The goal of pastoral planning is "that the patient will find inner peace with oneself, with one's surroundings and with God." This goal may never be far from the chaplain's mind. In this process, however, the chaplain needs to evaluate and prioritize the obstacles that stand in its way. In the final analysis, inner peace is God's gift. Hence there is a temptation to draw

God into the picture as soon as possible. We may not overlook that God usually does not work independently from the person but guides and stimulates in proportion to the patient's personal investment in the search. Consequently, the chaplain's approach needs to focus on the perspective that the patient is called to be one principle of operation with God. Every effort to gain self-esteem and self-confidence brings the patient one step closer to peace in a collaborative openness to God's presence.

A pastoral treatment plan is a process and needs to be flexible. The patient's condition and attitude is subject to many changes, and roads toward progress have many hills and valleys. The important factor is that the minister develop a plan of action, based upon the spiritual needs discussed on pages 61–64. Such a plan of action must stay in tune with the changing condition of the patient. It is best established in consultation and cooperation with the patient. Ultimately, it is his or her life and happiness that is at stake. A patient needs to come to the insight that the condition is incurable and that the only way to find peace is to integrate it into one's life-style rather than deny or fight it. Such integration is possible even if patients keep fighting against any infection that comes along. Integration means working at one's fullest capacity toward the wholeness of one's being. This goal guides the patient in his/her effort and must take both the assessment and the pastoral goal seriously.

Pastoral planning for persons with AIDS may need more flexibility than for any other disease because patients with AIDS are little inclined to stay in the hospital, even if they are allowed. They are in and out so frequently that a stable course of care is difficult. It is quite possible that a pastoral plan must include a long and slow developmental process. The rebuilding of their personality is made more difficult because of the religious rejection, real or imagined, that many have experienced. Pastoral planning for persons with AIDS must include more than an average dose of re-establishment of human relationships. However, once such human relationships begin to form, the natural tendency to relate to God will soon influence their lives. The back and forth relationship between human concern and relationship to God has to be a constant feature, since these two are so closely related.

The assessment instrument can be a helpful tool in the planning process. Once the chaplain has determined for his own records where the patient seems to be at that moment, this first evaluation can easily be updated through color-coding or through other methods that show the ups and downs of the progress. Such recording will help the chaplain to recognize the pitfalls for each patient as well as the encouraging and strengthening steps that contributed to real progress and inner peace. This personal recording allows the constant involvement of the patient with the chaplain.

Pastoral planning needs to include the perspective that humanity is created in the image of God. This means that humanity is called to translate God's love and goodness into the language of human behavior. Without rebuilding the human dimension, the translation of the divine into human expression will always fail.

C. Patients with Multiple Sclerosis

The Assessment

Earlier I indicated that the physical disabilities related to multiple sclerosis affect self-confidence, self-esteem, and the sense of value for oneself and toward society. This personal and relational stress is part of their present condition. Its presence must be acknowledged, but it does not have to drag a person down.

Although the illness means an almost uncontrollable and constant deterioration, patients still need to learn to focus on their strengths that still exist, not on what they have lost, even though their abilities may fluctuate considerably. Because of the fluctuating nature of the illness, it becomes important for the patient to understand the disease as thoroughly as possible. Such knowledge may have a discouraging effect upon some persons, but in general it will help the patient not to be taken by surprise and to be prepared for continuous adaptation. The irreversible downhill slide makes it difficult to maintain one's motivation. The integration of a strong personal value system with spiritual (nonmaterial) motives needs to be developed and supported.

The Pastoral Response

The hardest aspect of MS is its irreversible, insidious, and relentless deterioration of several physical faculties, such as walking, seeing, and others. The basis of a pastoral response in these conditions lies in supporting and strengthening the self-image of the patient and to assist the patient to accept his or her condition as a new challenge rather than as a deterioration. The focus needs to stay on what one can do, not on what one cannot do anymore. For some persons a sense of humor about the inability to perform certain activities can be an effective defense mechanism that does not deny the reality but refuses to be discouraged by it. The family who lives with the patient plays an important role in the process of pastoral care. They can see to it that no unreasonable demands are placed on such patients. Thus they acknowledge the condition of the patient. An understanding of the limitations and psychological pain caused by the illness is the beginning of the necessary support.

The Pastoral Planning

The planning for patients with MS is usually long-range planning. The request for assistance, however, will most likely come only when serious limitations are experienced. Between the episodes when MS flares up, patients usually will not show any desire to discuss the matter.

The most effective support is to be found in ways to maintain and further develop the patient's self-image and concept of self-value, independent from physical abilities. The acceptance of everyday occurrences can be very important. I think of Eric's mother who is in progressive stages of multiple sclerosis. She used to be an excellent cook, but it just does not work anymore. She suggested to Eric that he go out with some friends for his birthday because she could not do the cooking as she used to. Eric's response was, "Never mind the gourmet dinner, Mom. The simple dinner you can make is better than the gourmet dinner I can buy somewhere else." This acceptance of reality, combined with Eric's love and respect for his mother, is a source of personal and spiritual strength and growth. Multiple sclerosis is an disease where daily relationships need to incorporate a pastoral dimension. Working with the family is an essential part of the chaplain's task when caring for patients with multiple sclerosis.

C. Patients with Amyotrophic Lateral Sclerosis

The Assessment

The increasing sense of inability affects the sense of self-esteem, confidence and respect. There is also a deep anxiety when faced with progressive paralysis. Patients with amyotrophic lateral sclerosis need to develop a self-image that passes beyond physical performance and is rooted in their dignity as a person. The personal shame about their condition that so frequently accompanies the illness is difficult to take away. The inability to feed themselves and take care of other personal needs is to be acknowledged and accepted as something normal, i.e., as belonging to the condition and not the fault of the patient. The patient and the family need to know this and accept it. The motivation to make of life what one can make of it in the circumstances is difficult to maintain since the prospect is always dark. The experience of constant family support is also a very significant part of pastoral care. The understanding of the pastoral and spiritual dimension of daily life plays a significant role.

The Pastoral Response

A pastoral response must relate primarily to the support, maintenance, and development of a sense of personal dignity and value, totally independent from physical abilities. To acknowledge the reality and to accept the unavoidable are important factors. Any response needs to strike a balance between realism and a positive outlook on life. Sometimes one may have to discuss with the patient the prospects and the prognosis of the disease in general and of this person in particular. Patients need to know that their present condition is not uncommon and that it belongs to the illness. To know that certain conditions are a "normal" part of the illness helps to take away the feeling of shame and self-blame. For patients with ALS self-acceptance AS PERSONS is extremely important for inner peace.

The Pastoral Planning

Amyotrophic lateral sclerosis is difficult to integrate into life. The increasing problems and the increasing loss of independence constantly push the limits of self-respect and self-confidence. They are a constant reminder of a slow dying process. The pastoral planning must integrate ways to support self-acceptance even in total dependence, and a trust in God who asks only to utilize those qualities that are available to us in whatever condition we are. Peter was close to sixty when he was diagnosed with ALS. Although his family had a very limited understanding of the illness, they did understand that their father's behavior had a very deep reason, because they knew him as a man who was always active and neat in all he did. They turned out to be the primary and most important pastoral workers. They conveyed the reality of dignity and respect. Pastoral planning needs to include working with the immediate surroundings. They too are in need of support to handle the slow process of deterioration that places constantly greater pressure on them.

B. Patients with a Serious Physical Handicap

The Assessment

The important difference between physical handicaps and other incurable illnesses is that handicaps by themselves do not lead to death as other illnesses eventually do. Here also, the development, rebuilding, maintenance, etc., of a strong self-respect and acceptance lies at the basis of the search for inner peace.

For proper assessment it is necessary to understand the meaning and place of the lost ability (hand, finger, leg, breast, etc.) for the individual. What is lost in their personal vision of self cannot be replaced, but other qualities may be able to substitute for what is lost. It was a strange experience when a gentleman, who had been a thalidomide baby, asked for my business card and accepted it with his foot. It was outright embarrassing when this same gentleman wrote me a letter, and his "footwriting" appeared to be considerably better than my handwriting. He had not lost any of his dignity and value despite the fact that he had no arms. Understanding of the loss, the self-acceptance beyond the physical, and a realistic view of life are basic requirements for the restoration of an inner peace.

The Pastoral Response

The pastoral response must include an acknowledgement of the condition of the patient as well as of the loss that he or she suffers. The experience of the loss is the starting point for the new journey. Since the loss is limited—arm, leg, foot, quadriplegic, etc.—there are always areas of strength left with which the person can work and which can be developed. This change from one focus on personal ability to another must not be taken lightly because it involves a very significant change and challenge in the patient's life. Personal dignity and strength, together with a sense of value that goes beyond the physical (i.e., acceptance by others and trust in God), must offer the courage to rebuild one's life. This was the case with Raymond who had broken his neck in a diving accident and was paralyzed from the neck down. The unbelievable courage and dedication of his fiancée carried him through the deepest crisis and allowed him to develop a deep sense of confidence and trust in God. It was a rare privilege and teaching experience to prepare that couple for marriage and to preside at their wedding in the Church. Raymond's physical disability had become a "natural" part of their relationship. They could love each other as they were and love the God whose love they lived in their own way.

The Pastoral Planning

Patients with a serious handicap offer the opportunity for constructive long-term planning. Their task is, more than other illnesses, to integrate their limitation into a new form of productive life. Patients with other incurable illnesses integrate their limitations into their life, but their life usually has a very limited future. With seriously handicapped persons, this can be quite different. They may have a long life ahead of them.

Pastoral planning seeks the inner peace and self-acceptance that goes far beyond rehabilitative retraining for a professional job or even training for a new job. Retraining must be based upon an inner peace in a person or create this inner peace so that he or she can experience their own dignity and feel acceptable despite the handicap. Patients need to experience that the loss of a faculty or function does not decrease the value of their person. What has changed in them is the manner in which they express their ability and their personal value. The value itself remains and can increase through personal dedication and self-application despite difficulties. The presence of a handicap allows such a person to experience simultaneously the limitations of one's existence and the ability to manifest God's goodness in the way they develop themselves. These two aspects need to stay alive in the minds of the patient, his or her family, and the pastoral worker.

Using the Assessment Instrument

In these discussions we have studied the nature of the instrument for spiritual assessment. Although it is most effective in the pastoral care of patients with incurable diseases, it can also be effectively used with short-term patients. The major reason is that the instrument is not a questionnaire to be filled out but rather a screen against which the chaplain can project the image that the patient produces in the chaplain's mind.

Throughout these discussions my focus has been on persons with incurable illnesses for the simple reason that they cannot "outgrow" their condition. They need to integrate whatever their condition is into the fabric of their daily lives. There is one category which I did not discuss, namely, the aging.

Old age is not a disease. It is a normal human development, but it is also an irreversible process that brings radical changes in human life, behavior, and attitudes. Quite often it is accompanied by illness, dependence, loss of control over one's life, seeming rejection, and other frightening conditions. Most of the general principles that we have discussed in relation to incurable illnesses also apply to situations resulting from old age. However, there are some differences that are important to keep in mind. In order not to classify old age among ordinary illnesses, I will now look at some of these differences.

The deeper meaning of aging is perhaps best expressed in Henry Nouwen's statement: "Aging does not have to be hidden or denied, but can be understood, affirmed and experienced as a process of growth by which the mystery of life is slowly revealed to us."[1] Every individual approaches this process in his or her own way. This was portrayed interestingly by two sisters whom I met. Both were in their eighties, but how different they were! The younger one was sad and lamented copiously about all the things she could do in the past but which she had lost the ability to do. She was so preoccupied with her earlier abilities that she had no time to enjoy any of the things she could still do.

The older one was just the opposite. Every little bit of strength she still had was activated in household, social visits, sports, discussion clubs, and whatever else she could get involved in. Her abilities had decreased enormously during the last decade, but she maintained that every minute she spent in lamenting about the ideal past was less time she had to enjoy the beauty of the present. In dealing with the elderly, the major point is to help them to accept and integrate what they are at this moment.

Losses in the aging process

Every person is different. Some people like to say that aging is a state of mind, or "You are just as old as you think you are." But whatever the state of mind may be, changes take place in every aging process. There are always losses. Some are personal, some are general. Some of the more general losses[2] are:

- A decreasing physical vitality or changes in one's general health. This may lead to isolation and loneliness;

- Unpleasant changes in one's external appearance;

- Less relevancy in society, the feeling of not being needed any more and possibly being excluded;

- Important and familiar roles diminish, and one must assume new (lesser) roles;

[1] Kemper, Mettler, Guiffre, and Matzek, *Growing Wiser. The Older Person's Guide to Mental Wellness* (Boise: Health Wise Publications, 1988) 75.

[2] Much of the following is inspired by J. Godderis, *Subjective Beleving van het Ouder worden: Psychologische en psychopathologische Kanttekeningen. Pastorale Gids, A II, 1* (Brussels: Verbond voor Verzorgings Instellingen, 1981).

- Certain cherished dreams move out of reach, original motivations tend to decrease and a certain dullness tries to take over.

People deal with these losses in many different ways. Some of the more common are:

- *Regression* = a tendency to fall back on a form of dependence that felt comfortable in the past. Often this is accompanied by a degree of nostalgia and re-living the ideals of the past. The inability to accept the present situation leads to depression and sometimes to paranoia, suspecting that others take advantage of their weakened condition.

- *Denial* of one's condition which encourages some elderly to be involved in activities that are inappropriate. It is a tendency to overcompensate in order to hide. They have to prove to the world that they are still with it.

- *Vicarious living.* The dreams that were not realized must now be lived out in their children or grandchildren. Unfortunately, this vicarious living pattern often leads to frustration, disappointment, and anger.

When people get older they become more susceptible to illnesses and heal more slowly than they used to. We can, therefore, expect in old people more illnesses, and the illnesses are much less curable than they were in the past.

A Pastoral Response

The above characteristics of the aging process help us to make an intelligent assessment of their personal and spiritual needs. Here, just as in patients with incurable illnesses, it is important to help the elderly find meaning in their present life and condition.

For persons who experience the loss of abilities or other losses, one might focus on dealing with the process of grieving.[3] But perhaps more important is the focus on the interhuman and social relationships as Hansson and Carpenter state: "Social functioning is integral to human functioning, not only because it leads to other desired outcomes, but because we crave and need contact with others."[4]

To keep elderly people informed about happenings in the family and neighborhood and to listen to their observations is a major step in contributing to their mental and spiritual health. James Fries points to the necessity of assisting older people to avoid learned helplessness and develop self-efficacy.[5] Such efforts may look more like counseling than pastoral care, yet the person who has a joy in life will also have the ability for a joyful surrender to God.

Since aging is frequently accompanied by illness, this combination places a strain on the chaplain's ingenuity. I will not try to give a formula to handle this. True pastoral care is an interpersonal exchange between patient and chaplain in which the willingness and ability to share the journey will determine the spiritual growth of patient and chaplain.

The method to use the instrument most effectively is to have for each patient, particularly for each patient who undergoes extended care, an individual instrument that the chaplain fills out after a visit with the patient. To fill out an instrument forms a basis and reference for further pastoral care. In the course of time, the chaplain will notice changes in the patient and, by marking the items of the instrument with colored pencils, the patient's road toward wholeness can be shown fairly accurately. This "charting" gives the chaplain an instrument for assessment and re-assessment. The charting of this development forces the chaplain to formulate, however tentatively, the spiritual course of the patient. It helps the chaplain to cor-

---

[3] Kemper, Mettler. Giuffre, Matzek, *Growing Wiser. The Older Person's Guide to Mental Wellness* (Healthwise, Inc., 1986) 77–83.

[4] Hansson, Robert O., and Carpenter, Bruce N., *Relationships in Old Age. Coping with the Challenge of Transition* (New York: Guilford Press, 1994) 2.

[5] James F. Fries, *Aging Well. A Guide for Successful Seniors* (New York: Addison-Wesley, 1989) 54–62.

rect and adapt the course of care according to the patient's needs and unfolding. Both in illness and aging the chaplain is called to be a friend and companion who shares the journey to God.

For the benefit of the user, I offer the following form for use in the office files.

Instrument for Spiritual Assessment

PATIENT'S NAME _____

DATE(S) OF CHARTING _____

Chaplain _____

1. How does the patient see the place of God in his or her life?

   a. Everything that happens in my life is explicitly willed by God.

   1   2   3   4   5

   b. God is sort of a partner in my life. He is involved in all that I do.

   1   2   3   4   5

   c. God is sitting on his throne high in the heavens with little concern about what goes on in human life.

   1   2   3   4   5

   d. God is more a demanding law-giver than a loving father.

   1   2   3   4   5

2. What is the main characteristic of the patient's attitude toward him or herself?

   a. A feeling of self-pity and/or disbelief that this could happen to him or her.

   1   2   3   4   5

   b. A feeling of self-rejection because all personal value is destroyed by the illness.

   1   2   3   4   5

   c. A feeling of inner peace and acceptance since he/she has handled many problems and God is always there as a partner and friend.

| 1 | 2 | 3 | 4 | 5 |

d. A feeling of anger with God and neighbor since all seem to have abandoned him/her.

| 1 | 2 | 3 | 4 | 5 |

3. How can the patient's relationship with family and friends best be described?

a. A relationship of trust and mutual support.

| 1 | 2 | 3 | 4 | 5 |

b. A relationship of mutual indifference.

| 1 | 2 | 3 | 4 | 5 |

c. A friendly relationship but without warmth or closeness.

| 1 | 2 | 3 | 4 | 5 |

d. A distant, mistrusting relationship in which the patient easily feels betrayed, rejected and abandoned.

| 1 | 2 | 3 | 4 | 5 |

4. What is the patient's understanding of and interest in prayer?

a. Total indifference since prayer has no meaning or benefit.

| 1 | 2 | 3 | 4 | 5 |

b. A means to ask (or plead with) God to give healing or at least to arrest the illness.

| 1 | 2 | 3 | 4 | 5 |

c. An angry rejection of prayer because despite all prayer the illness continues to ravage his/her health.

| 1 | 2 | 3 | 4 | 5 |

d. A source of strength which enables the patient to find union with God and consolation in suffering.

1   2   3   4   5

5. What is the main characteristic of the patient's attitude toward his or her religious community or church?

a. A feeling of respect and trust because of the community's/Church's support.

1   2   3   4   5

b. A feeling of anger because of the Church's indifference or the Church's rejection of my situation.

1   2   3   4   5

c. Complete indifference because the church has nothing to offer.

1   2   3   4   5

d. An inner desire to belong to the Church and be supported by it, but also a deep-seated fear of rejection.

1   2   3   4   5

Chaplain's observations:

_____

_____

_____

_____

_____

_____

_____

_____